Fundamental Elements of Physical Education

Dr. M.L. Kamlesh
M.A. (English), M.Ed. (Phy. Edn)., Ph.D., D.Sc. (Sri Lanka)
Former Principal,
Lakshmi National College of Physical Education,
Thiruvananthipuram (Kerala)
&
Former Dean, Faculty of Physical Education,
University of Kerala

KSK PUBLISHERS & DISTRIBUTORS
7/26, Basement, Ansari Road, Darya Ganj,
New Delhi-110002.

Published by:

KSK PUBLISHERS & DISTRIBUTORS

7/26, Basement, Ansari Road, Darya Ganj, New Delhi-110002.

Ph.: (O) 011-65190343, 43551324, 42564726
(M) 8459074169, 9811088729, (Fax) 011-42564726
(Res.) 47091605

E-mail: khelsahitya1@rediffmail.com

Web: www.khelsahitya.com

I.S.B.N. - 978-81-89983-37-6

PRINTED IN INDIA 2014
RE- PRINT 2022

Laser Typeset by:
JAIN MEDIA GRAPHICS
Delhi-110035.

Printed by:
ASIAN OFFSET PRINTERS
Delhi

Preface

Introduction of physical education as a subject at the school level of education in several states has undoubtedly boosted the development of it as a profession. Now that more and more universities are coming forward to offer physical education, health and sport as an elective/optional subject at the undergraduate level is really a very firm step in the right direction, giving a further uplift to the sport an physical activity programmes for the youth. A few universities have already accomplished this great job with good amount of success but unless this subject becomes a "required" programme, the real benefits to the students and the community at large might not come. So there is a need to take this on an urgent basis. The National Sports Policy and National Education Policy also talk of integrating sport and physical education with the "learning experience" in the educational institutions. The framers of these policies may deserve complements from the physical education and sport fraternity for the vision shown but too slow progress in this regard is certainly a cause for anxiety, which needs to be immediately addressed.

Physical education is a very vast subject and its theoretical framework contains some fundamental and greatly applied knowledge of a large variety of science and art subjects such as physiology, biomechanics, psychology, management, anthropometry, history, and so on. It is just not possible, nor advisable, to impart knowledge to a common multitude of students in all these subjects in a single go because much of the content is for the consumption of the students of professional physical education courses at the colleges/ university departments of physical education. So, the focus in this book has been on a few fundamental elements of physical education the understanding of which is generally considered important for the students of undergraduate courses in different faculties at the universities. Even the school students and those undergoing the short and/or lower level professional courses such as certificate in physical education may benefit a lot from this humble effort. An attempt has been made to keep the standard of information almost within the grasp of the students and in a language easily understood by them without sacrificing the literary standards. The Hindi rendering of this book has already hit the market and has been received well. In bringing out this English version, a little addition/subtraction in the content has been made which need not be a cause of anxiety; for example, basic information on National Sports Policy and National Sport Awards has been given in the appendices.

Shri Vivek Thani of the Khel Sahitya, New Delhi deserves all the kudos for coming forward to publish this terse volume with all the usual enthusiasm and a good businessman like approach for the benefit of the students and teachers of physical education in the country. Thanks are also due to all those who have been helpful in the preparation of this book and the students - both past and present - who are a perennial source of inspiration to me in all my writing endeavours.

Patiala,
October, 2010

M.L. Kamlesh

CONTENTS

CHAPTER: ONE

EDUCATION AND PHYSICAL EDUCATION

Learning, Education and Movement Education

Of all the creatures known or seen around or the ones that can be conceived of, man is the only living being which is most educable. It is so, because Nature has blessed man with the innate equipment of intelligence - a superior brain and a complex nervous system - that can absorb external information, store it and use it as per demands of the situation. Like other animals, man is also born with such behaviours as instincts, emotions, and reflexes that make his survival possible and also enable him to struggle for his own existence and that of the fellow beings. However, unlike animals, man does not remain slave of his instincts through out life because he is capable of learning thousands of things and reduce his dependence on his native behaviour. After birth, as man interacts with his environment variedly and meaningfully, he not only becomes capable of learning how to modify and refine his instinctive behaviour but also acquire new modes, manners and patterns of behaviour, e.g. motor, work, sport, conceptual and social skills; knowledge, habits, social norms, etiquettes, etc. We call this process *learning* - the most important attribute of man, and which makes man truly human and enable him to look apart from animals. Learning is basic to man and is the foundation of education. The scope both for education and learning in man's life knows no limits. It is undeniable fact that there can virtually be no education without learning. As human beings learn, they educate themselves also. The end-product of learning is education. Every one - high low, rich, poor, man, woman, old and young - keep on learning one thing or the other through life, thereby making education an unending process. Without learning and education human beings would be no better than animals. Education is the most valuable asset of the cultured man.

As there is no end to the development of mind, so there is no finish-line in learning and in educating oneself. Every thing that we do (or we are impressed upon to do) formally or informally, and which makes our behaviour *change* in some way is learning, and learning that provides us with an elevated status in life is education. From learning to pronounce the first syllable in infancy to becoming a celebrity in literature, science or sport later in life or from toddling on fours to piloting an airplane in adulthood falls within the purview of education. Interestingly, education is not confined to the four walls of the classroom in a school or a college, but it is a universally wide phenomenon that gives us opportunities for developing different abilities and puts us on a higher plane of thought, action, conduct and character. The inevitable process of education starts at home with the mother and other members of the family taking care of child's needs and along with it teaching him things like language, communication, physical and mental skills; reading, writing, playing, solving personal problems, and so on.

An analysis of the human development process shows that man's basic or life education begins with the growth of motor skills – locomotion, crawling, creeping, toddling, sitting, standing, walking, running, jumping, throwing, hitting, kicking, etc. Mother Nature has well-sequenced child's motor skill development. It allows things to happen on priority and in such a manner that one thing (skill or trait) leads to another without any one's knowledge so that the child keeps moving up the ladder with assured and steady steps. Experts call it ***movement education***, which, in good quality, adequate measure, and varied form ensures the development of physical qualities such as strength, speed, accuracy, flexibility, agility, coordinative abilities, and so on. This, in turn, becomes the cause of child's mental development. It has now become an established fact that in order to be mentally sharp, emotionally stable and intellectually bright, the child must exercise his limbs regularly and vigorously, for the muscles are the *instruments of intelligence*. Today, scientists know for sure that muscle and mind are closely related.

While Charles Darwin's Evolutionary Theory underlines the fact that activity is the basis of growth and development, Aristotle's concept of *sound mind in sound body* virtually emphasizes that physical development is foundational to all other types of development - mental, intellectual, moral and social. Socrates, Plato, and Aristotle considered play, sport, and physical activity as the basis of all education; so they made these as an integral part of child's education right from the tender age. For the ancient Greeks complete education meant aesthetics, ethics, mathematics and athletics. Body is the basis of human existence; man's all life functions depend upon it. It must, therefore, be cared for properly i.e. kept healthy, fit and strong through regular vigorous physical activity apart from proper nutrition and healthy environment - so important for health, fitness and wellbeing. A truly educated person must first of all be healthy and strong so as to resist disease, perform his routines without undue fatigue; and must still be left with enough energy to meet emergencies. The relationship between learning, education and movement education, i.e. physical education is perfect. Man without education and education without physical education are a sheer waste.

MEANING & DEFINITION OF EDUCATION AND PHYSICAL EDUCATION

Education and physical education are no two different phenomena; they are two aspects of the same process - education of man which has its aim as harmonious development of human personality. People with a restricted vision, think that education means learning of 3Rs (reading, writing and arithmetic). In their view, classroom teaching is everything because by collecting knowledge about the things around by reading books and listening to teachers' lectures, a student prepares himself to face life. In fact, education is much more than classroom learning. It is a vast field of human experience and interaction in which the child acquires a large variety of physical, mental, communicative, interactive skills, and human relationships largely by self-effort, observation of and participation in the real drama of life. Learning motor, skills, activity skills and skills of games and sports is a basic aspect of education and all other things come later. It is wrong to think of physical education something distant as well as different from education. As it is impossible to truncate man into body and mind, so also it is difficult to divide education into physical education and mental education. When we talk of education, we talk of education as a whole inclusive of physical, mental, intellectual and social education. No physical skill can be acquired without the involvement of mind in the learning process and no mental skill can be learned and mastered without the active involvement of muscles – both gross and fine – wholly or partially as the situation dictates. In fact, there is no dividing line between what is physical and what is mental; it is only a question of emphasis on one or the other element of an activity or experience, and the quantum of nerve or muscle movement involved in a particular skill. Chess and billiard are more of mental activities, while soccer, hockey or gymnastics more physical.

Meaning and Definition of Education

The word *education* is derived from Latin E*ducare* (meaning to 'bring up') or *Educere* indicating *drawing out* or *bringing forth*. Therefore, education, in its simplest meaning, is better understood as a process by which the teacher tries to draw out what is best in the child, as Mahatma Gandhi believed. In concise Oxford Dictionary education is defined as *learning that takes place in schools or school-like environments (formal education) or in the world at large; the transmission of the values and accumulated knowledge of a society*. In developing cultures there is often little formal education; children learn from their environment and activities, and the adults around them act as teachers. In more complex societies, where there is more knowledge to be passed on, a more selective and efficient means of transmission - the school and teacher-becomes necessary. Most educationists agree that education actually means affording fullest opportunities to the growing children to unfold their potential to the maximum possible extent and thrusting any thing on them from outside. A few definitions of education may make the concept of education clear:

> Education must make the boys and girls to be fearless, free and open minded, self-reliant, full of the spirit of enquiry and self-criticism...
>
> *- Rabindranath Tagore*
>
> Education is not the amount of information that is put into the brain running riot there, but it is the assimilation of ideas..., it should give us character that would make us flower into the best of humans...
>
> *- Swami Vivekananda*
>
> Education is the process of living through a common reconstruction of experiences. It is the development of all those capacities in the individual which enable to control his environment and fulfill his possibilities.
>
> *- John Dewey*
>
> Education means a natural, progressive and systematic development of man's all innate powers.
>
> *- Pestalozzi*
>
> Education is the complete development of the individuality of the child so that he can make an original contribution to human life according to the best of his capacity.
>
> *- T. P ercy Numn*

Education may mean many things to many people for it has been viewed from a variety of angles for ages. However, the essence of education lies in a few fundamental truths inherent in its definitions given by great educationists, philosophers, and others. Precisely, all education, under all cultural-social circumstances, must aim to:

- draw out the best in man in terms of his innate genetic potential;
- develop human character and personality to their fullest extent;

- prepare the individual for struggle in life by helping him or her develop such abilities as show him or her strong and self-reliant;
- offer opportunities for the child to be creative as well as critical in his or her approach towards life; and
- inculcate in every child social, ethical and human values, discipline and a sense of patriotism.

Aim of Education

Swami Vivekananda very rightly had said that 'the real education is that which prepares a man for struggle in life. It prepares him for social service, develops his character, and finally imbues him with the spirit and courage of a lion. Any other education is worse than useless'. In real sense of the term, it is proper education that lifts man from the state of an animal, illuminates his mind, enlightens his intellect and shapes up his personality.

The aim of education is directly related to the philosophy of life and life values which the society cherishes most at any point of time. Great people always have a much wider vision of life while setting the aim of education. According to Painter, the aim of education is *complete development* meaning development of the child in all important aspects of personality. The great spiritual philosopher Shankaracharya said that the 'ultimate aim of education is to prepare the child for the realization of *moksha* (salvation)'. An eminent educational psychologist James Ross set the aim of education as *development of valuable personality and spiritual individuality*. In Froebel's view, the task of education is to "assist natural development towards its destined end". "The chief aim of education," said Shri Aurobindo, "should be to help the growing soul to draw out that in itself, which is best and make it perfect for a noble use".

Major Objectives of Education

Charles A. Bucher, a well-known physical educationist enumerated a number of objectives of education and classified them into four major groups.

Objectives of Self-Realization

These objectives include an enquiring mind, knowledge of diseases and health, family and community health, skill as a participant and-spectator in sport, resources of utilizing leisure hours in mental pursuits, appreciation of beauty, and directing one's life towards worthwhile goals.

Objectives of Human Relationship

These objectives pertain to success and happiness in life and include human relationship and human welfare, a rich social experience through play, play cooperatively with others, courtesy, fair play and sportsmanship, and good family and home living.

Objectives of Economic Efficiency

Under this group fall such objectives as education for good workmanship, education for vocational placement, education for successful work, education for professional growth, and education for wise consumption of goods and services.

Objectives of Civic Responsibility

These objectives include education for humanitarianism, education for tolerance, education for conformance with laws, education for civic responsibility, and education for democratic living.

The Indian Education Commission (1964) considered education as "a powerful instrument of social, economic, and cultural transformation, necessary for realization of the national goals". Further, the Patel Committee on Education (1977) observed: "The objectives of education should enable an individual to acquire knowledge, skills, habits, attitudes, and values necessary for (1) a successful performance of responsibility as a citizen, and (2) a rewarding personal life by the development of (a) innate talents, (b) powers of creative enterprise, and (c) the capacity to appreciate the splendour of life revealed from communion with nature, and man with man."

Meaning and Definition of Physical Education

Most people know physical education by its earliest name – PT or physical training, and the in-charge of this activity programme at school is lovingly nick-named as PT or drill master or PT sir. Knowledgeable people call it physical exercise which is defined as 'a process of bodily movements in a particular way'. Physical training is, more or less, a formal way of physical conditioning generally with an aim to make the body tough and resilient. Common people engage in physical exercise in order to sharpen appetite or to jerk out large muscles of the body after a tiring or a monotonous daily routine.

Over the decades, this narrow concept of physical exercise has undergone a sea change and today physical education is the correct expression for what was earlier called as physical training. It needs to be known that physical training is merely a set of graded exercises done for certain purposes in a certain setting, but physical education is more than merely movements of the bodily muscles and joints in a given sequence; it is education of man through the medium of various physical activities.

Physical education is a comparatively recent expression for various physical activity programmes carried out in school, college or else where, as an educational experience. The word physical refers to body and underlines such bodily qualities as strength, speed, stamina, endurance, co-ordination, flexibility, movement etc., considered basic to health and fitness for work or sport in general. Education may mean any thing to any one but when used in combination with physical, it is understood to be a process through which one educates himself physically and ensures harmonious development of personality.

Physical education today has been accepted as a curricular activity and an integral component of learning experience at school education level to begin with. In fact, it is the most practical aspect of education because it is rooted in the principle of *learning by doing*. The most important fundamental process of education begins with play-way education or movement education, which lays and solidifies the foundation for all kinds of learning and education later in life.

Definition

Modern definitions of physical education mainly come from the Western scholars because in Europe and United States, play, sport, recreation, exercise, etc., enjoy parity with other academic subjects in schools and colleges. In all advanced countries, movement education is the beginning of all education.

According to Charles A. Bucher "Physical education is an integral part of the total education process and has its aim the development of physically, mentally, emotionally, and socially fit citizens through the medium of physical activities which have been selected with a view to realizing these outcomes". In Irwin's view: "Physical education is a program of physical activities that develops health in youth through various organic systems; it develops skills in physical activities which have implication for enjoyment, emotional development, recreation and the optimum development of the human organism". Jay B. Nash referred to physical education as "... that field of education which deals with big muscle activities and the related responses". Jesse Feiring Williams claimed: "Physical education is the sum of man's physical activities selected as to kind and conducted as to outcomes". For Lumpkin, "Physical education is a process through which an individual obtains optimal physical, mental and social skills and fitness through physical activity". Harold M. Barrow & Janie P. Brown defined physical education as "an education of and through human movement where many of the educational objectives are achieved by means of big muscle activities involving sports, games, gymnastics, dance, and fitness activities". There is a general agreement among people that physical education is education through the physical and of not the physical.

The Indian perspective of modern physical education is reflected in the *National Plan of Physical Education and*

Recreation (1956):

> Physical education is education. It is education through physical activities for the development of the total personality of the child to its fullness and perfection in body, mind and spirit.

It is immediately concerned with organic fitness and such other outcomes as would help the individual develop into a balanced personality. The common points of agreement in various definitions of physical education may be summed up as under:

- Physical education is an integral part of education.
- The aim and objectives of education and physical education are in no way at variance.
- In physical education, big muscle activity is the sole medium of physical and related development.
- Physical education aims at harmonious development of personality.
- Organic development, motor fitness and health are major objectives and concerns of physical education at all levels of education.
- Play, games, sports, dance, gymnastics, etc., constitute the core of physical education programme.
- Intellectual, moral, emotional and social aspects of development emerge from interactivity among children on the playing fields.

AIM AND OBJETIVES OF PHYSICAL EDUCATION

Aim

Aim is a *general statement of the highest purpose* of an endeavour, enterprise or a programme. Objectives are *concrete, solid, specific and achievable steps or goals*, the achievement of which leads one to aim - the final destination. They can be likened to the small tributaries that feed a river. While the aim is one, objectives may be many and diverse. The aim reflects the ideal, the objectives reflect reality principles. The ideal contained in the statement 'harmonious development of human personality to its fullness and perfection in body, mind and spirit', exemplifies aim; motor fitness, organic efficiency, morality, emotional stability etc., exemplify objectives as they are measurable *qualities* or *attributes* of personality.

Importantly, the aim and objectives - of education and physical education - draw the inspirational and material stuff from the cultural, political, social and economic philosophy of a nation or community, and are influenced by the changes occurring in society from time to time. It needs to be noted that great gymnastic movements, fitness drives, physical culture campaigns, etc., have played an important role in (a) mobilizing public opinion for healthful living, and (b) bringing about political and social revolutions in several countries at various periods of history. Physical education today is getting highly sport-oriented because winning gold medals in the Olympic Games and other international competitions has come to be considered as a matter of national prestige and individual excellence almost every where. The 'general well-being' objective is now a secondary motive of all physical education programmes. Sport has become the chief focus for physical education, and a great attraction in politics and even in economics. But sport is not for all; it is for a *gifted* few. For a common man health and fitness are matters of basic concern. Thanks to the television due to which there is enough much-needed awareness about health and fitness among the masses. More and more people are now motivated to take regular physical exercise in order to keep fit, strong and vibrant.

India is a sovereign secular democratic republic. Its national physical education programme, as enunciated in the National Sports Policy -2001, offers equal opportunities for all irrespective of caste, creed, religion, and language to develop such physical, mental, intellectual, social and moral qualities as will enable them to become true sons of the motherland and uphold values of a great democratic nation. The ideal is perfectly in line with the general aim of education. Jesse Feiring Williams proposed the following aim of physical education:

> Physical education should aim to provide skilled leadership, adequate facilities and ample time that will afford an opportunity for the individuals and the groups to act in situations that are physically wholesome, mentally stimulating and satisfying, and socially sound.

The emphasis in this statement has been laid on the all-round development of human personality by providing to all without exception equal opportunity for participation in various productive physical activities under competent leadership. According to the National Plan of Physical Education and Recreation (1956) the aim of physical education "must be to make every child physically, mentally, emotionally fit and also to develop in him such personal and social qualities as will help him to live happily with others and build him up as a good citizen". In short, as an organized and well-planned programme of physical activity, physical education must strive to develop the personality of each and every individual in harmony with highest ideals of a democratic education.

Objectives

The objectives - *specific statements of purposes* - of physical education, often called goals are found in a great variety and number, and may be categorized into several groups. Dr. Jay B. Nash put the objectives of physical education into four distinct groups as given below:

1. *Organic Development Objectives:* Physical prowess resulting from participation in big muscle/ motor activity
2. *Neuromuscular Development Objectives:* Control over body's mechanisms, ability to cut down waste motions
3. *Interpretative Development Objectives:* Power of judgment, ability to interpret and face and situations

4. *Emotional Development Objectives:* Drive for action, confidence, success and sense of belonging

The American Association for Health, Physical Education and Recreation (1965) listed the following major purposes of physical education:

- To help children move in a skilled and effective manner in all selective activities in which they engage in the physical education program, and also in those situations that they will experience during their life time.
- To develop an understanding and appreciation of movements in children and youth so that their lives will become more meaningful, purposeful and productive.
- To develop an understanding and appreciation of certain scientific principles concerned with movement that relate to such factors as time, space, force and mass relationships.
- To develop through games and sports better interpersonal relationships.
- To develop the various organic systems of the body so that they will respond in a healthful way to the increasing demands placed on them.

The objectives of physical education enumerated in the National Plan of physical Education and Recreation may be charted out and explained as follows:

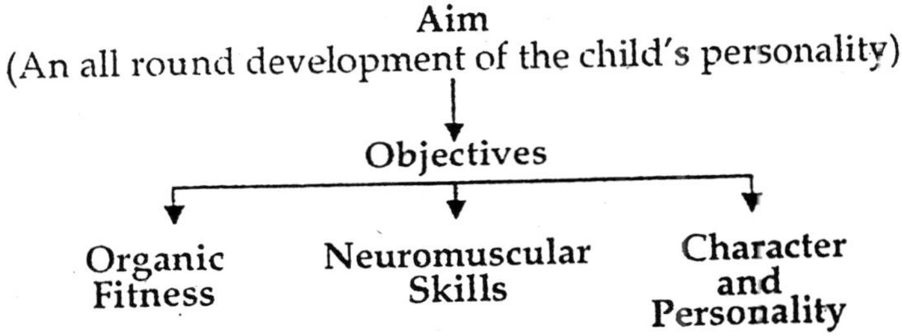

Organic Fitness Objectives.

These objectives include development of good posture of sitting, standing, walking, running etc., a reasonable level of fitness, ability to postpone fatigue, good amount of muscular strength, endurance, sound health, and efficiency of various organ-systems. The achievement of these objectives will enable the individual to resist disease, perform one's duties without unduly getting fatigued and enjoy blessings of Nature. Life is miserable without organic fitness; human survival depends solely on it. Apart from balanced diet, an unpolluted and invigorating environment, regular exercise is a necessary condition for developing right kind and high level of fitness. Greater emphasis now being placed on competitive sport makes it all the more necessary for the athletes to test very high on performance-related or motor fitness. Man's success - whether in life or in sport - squarely depends on fitness. Therefore, physical education, on the whole, should strive to provide opportunity to every one - young and old, men or women, athletes and non-athletes, service and business people, etc. - to develop fitness, measure the level of their fitness periodically and improve upon their existing standard. Fitness is a must to ensure human security, efficiency and productivity. A fit person is an asset to the nation, the weak is a liability on himself, on his family and on his nation. The fit commands and the unfit demands, the fit survives and dominates, and the fit stands as a rock in the thick of the storm and the unfit goes to the wall.

Organic fitness is a relative term. Age, sex, occupation, life-style etc., are its limiting factors. A wide variety of fitness enhancing methods - ranging from simple jogging to weight training - is now available to suit every one's requirement.

Neuromuscular Skills

Fitness and organic efficiency are closely related to motor (neuromuscular) development of a child. Nerves and muscles are the chief instruments of movement - both internal (physiological functioning) and external (observable activities of walking, running, jumping, etc). In infancy and childhood, learning begins with motor activity. Gradually as the motor control spreads from large muscles to fine muscles, the rate and quality of motor-skill acquisition increase enormously. Stages of growth and sequences of motor development move up the course hand in hand, the natural creeping, crawling, toddling, standing, walking, running, catching, and throwing movement patterns serving as stepping stones for development of more complex skills of hitting, kicking, passing, chipping, shooting, dribbling, etc. The more productively does a child interact with the environment the better is the quality of his motor control and neuromuscular coordination. In nature, this is a well-established law. Biologists have traced the growth of mind to motor activity only, arguing that muscular movement is the very basis of motor behaviour.

Man would not be able to develop intelligence without the well-coordinated functioning of muscles and nerves. From pushing a hand cart to piloting a supersonic plane, from throwing a stone at the mango tree to scoring a basket, and from drawing a crude circle to painting a portrait, we learn thousands of neuromuscular skills with increasing degree of complexity. The relationship between neuromuscular skills and cognitive development, intelligence, emotions and intellectual ability is found to be almost perfect. People deficient in neuromuscular skills find themselves out of place almost every where - at school, at home, at club and elsewhere - and encounter variety of problems of adjustment in life. There is no better way of acquiring diverse neuromuscular skills than to participate in play, exercise, and sports and games. Physical activity facilitates and strengthens neuromuscular coordination resulting in perfect body-mind integration. Physical education programme must lay the greatest stress on the development of neuromuscular coordination skills at all growth stages.

Character and Personality Development

These objectives include the development of moral and personal qualities that constitute character and personality. Importantly, when children participate in recreational activities and competitive sports and games, they are likely to imbibe such qualities as confidence, courage, team spirit, sense of right and wrong, fair play, tolerance, risk-taking, tough-mindedness, cooperation, comradeship, sportsmanship, positive social attitudes, etc. While character primarily denotes moral and ethical qualities and is a matter of subjective judgment, personality is much wider in dimensions and objective in outlook. Mental, intellectual, spiritual, emotional and social ingredients of personality are as important as its physical aspect in magnitude. Physical activity programmes offer immense opportunity for the individuals and the groups to interact with one another purposefully, influence one another and be influenced in a variety of ways, and optimize the learning process, which serves as a good measuring yardstick for personality and character development. Sociologists believe that a balanced and stable personality emerges from a sustained social interaction among people on the play fields - both as participants and as spectators. Play has a cathartic effect on human emotions, and play fields level off racial, political, social, economic, and cultural inequalities among people. It is important to learn to be sportspersons first and last.

Games and sports strengthen democratic process and create an environment in which the audience and actors have to become fully aware of their responsibilities, rights and duties as members of a responsible nation and human society. Physical education must uphold human values and strengthen human relationships. Strong characters and well-groomed personalities must evolve out from sport and activity experiences on the play fields, in the gymnasiums and the swimming pools.

MODERN CONCEPT OF PHYSICAL EDUCATION

Until Independence in 1947, physical education in our country was generally known as physical training. In schools, the *PT period* was handled by the physical training instructors who generally were ex-army personnel, and often gave lessons in some not very well-sequenced physical exercises, and army-type drill and marching. They managed the physical activity show with regimented command and military precision, often using disciplining stick.

In India, the era of *modern* physical education began in 1920 with the establishment of YMCA College of Physical Education at Madras, following by several colleges in various parts of the country during 1930s and a new generation of trained physical education teachers appeared on the scene. Besides physical training exercises and drill and marching, the teaching of games and sports began to be organized for the talented and motivated students after school hours. So physical education, though an extra-curricular activity, turned a new leaf at the hands of *skill masters* who knew a good bit of theory and practical activities.

Today, the situation has globally changed a great deal. We look at physical education, not merely as a physical exercise programme necessary for keeping good health and improving fitness but also as an academic (scientific) discipline with emphasis on research and methodological development, and a profession that offers job opportunities to millions and avenues for service to the society. All the three aspects of physical education collectively focus on human welfare and harmonious development of human personality. The guiding principles of physical education as an academic discipline come from various sciences such as anatomy, physiology, kinesiology, bio-mechanics, psychology, sociology, anthropology, etc., as well as humanities dealing with human "experience, insight, and understanding".

Movement or activity is a complex phenomenon. It is a subject of research, debate and discussion under a variety of science and art disciplines. The unprecedented growth in competitive sport and unimaginably improving human performance in all sports without exception these days is being attributed to the application of scientific principles in the training of athletes, construction of sport infrastructure and manufacture of athletic gear and equipment including the footwear and sportswear. Most professional practices of the physical education teachers derive their strength and substance from sustained research in such areas as material and human management, teaching methodology, behavioural and life sciences, humanities, and so on. Physical education, as a profession, is well placed in the system of education and the physical educators enjoy parity in status, career advancement avenues, work load, etc., with other teachers at all levels of education.

The physical education teacher of the 21st century, therefore, has to play diversified roles of a teacher, a coach, a scientist, a researcher, an organizer, and a manager. So profound is the impact of the *emerging sport sciences* on the theories and practices of physical education that a variety of new titles is being proposed and even used in universities abroad such as Science of Human Movement, Movement Arts and Sciences, Movement Education, Kinesiology, Sports Education, Development Motor Performance, etc. Modern physical education is no simple programme of physical activity, play, recreation or a means of "sharpening appetite", it is a science of *educating* every participant how to live most and perform best with due deference to one's ability, interest, aptitude and potential.

SCOPE OF PHYSICAL EDUCATION

In its modern concept, physical education is a multi-dimensional field of human experience. As an academic subject, it is an integral part of the school and college curricula and deals with the most important aspect of life - the human movement. It offers immense scope for research in motor skill learning, behavioural sciences, biomechanics, material and human resource management in activity and sport, organizational skills, teaching methodology, training regimens, etc., as they relate to health, fitness and performance. In its professional perspective, physical education is a teacher education and contributes a cadre of competent teachers for all levels of education – schools, colleges, universities, etc. – coaches and sports scientists who serve the society in different capacities. With diversification of courses coming up fast, fitness trainers or fitness centre managers are a new feather in the cap of physical education as a profession.

In its simplest form, physical education offers a well-planned programme of physical activity for school and college students, and people in general. Whether curricular or non-curricular (informal, recreational), the activity programme of physical education is marked by variety and diversity to suit all tastes and needs of the people. Precisely, several groups of activities are today part and parcel of the body of physical education activities.

- *Games & Sports*: The bulk of physical education comprises of skill-based individual sports like archery, athletics, swimming, boxing, judo, wrestling, shooting, gymnastics, etc., and team sports such as badminton, tennis, table tennis, basketball, volleyball, hockey, handball, football, kabaddi, kho-kho, etc. In order to become just proficient and achieve some excellence in at least one of these games/sports one requires years of organized learning, practice and competitive experience. In physical education programme, these activities are used both as recreation and as competition for testing powers of the human body and mind.
- *Minor Games*: Tag games, minor games, relays, lead-up games, recreational games and small area games come in an endless variety, suiting all age groups and the two genders in almost all activity situations and occasions. Apart from the fun and recreation they provide, they also help strengthen the skills of various major sports and games played on competitive basis. Much of the movement education for elementary and primary sections of a school is based on these activities.

- ***Self-defence Activities***: Dual and mass combats like wrestling, boxing, judo, karate, stunts, stick, dagger fight, etc. – both in original form as martial arts and in modified form as sports – have an important place in physical education programme especially for school children. They enable the participants to develop such qualities of character as confidence, courage, determination, dominance, fighting spirit, daring, sympathy, fair play, tolerance, sportsmanship, quick decision-making, etc.
- ***Gymnastics***: Considered as a *mother sport* along with athletics and swimming, gymnastics is an exceptionally effective means of developing basic fitness components such as agility, flexibility, balance, coordination, strength and speed as well as body poise, grace and beauty. In fact, all sporting activity starts with some kind of gymnastic acrobatics. Gymnastics has no parallel as far educational and aesthetic values of physical activity are concerned. In schools and colleges, gymnastic programme is limited to floor and apparatus exercises for two sexes.
- ***Recreation***: Any thing and every thing we do for fun and enjoyment is recreation - play, sport, hobbies, adventure, music, painting, fishing, dancing, etc. In fact, the activities that enable us to reduce or eliminate monotony, boredom and fatigue arising out of life routines or work fall within the orbit of recreation especially when these are organized under competent leadership. Factory workers, labouring class, business executives, intellectuals, professionals, etc. – all need to engage in some form of recreational activity or leisure hour pastimes to relax their tense nerves after day's work.
- ***Correctives***: Therapeutic, corrective and rehabilitative exercises play a crucial role in removing physical deformities (defects) with which several

children in schools are afflicted, and seriously injured sportspersons. They help rectify clumsy movements. The corrective movements improve our physical structure and function so that we have a better carriage (posture) making our looks more impressive and smart. Rehabilitative exercises put the inured athletes back on the track quickly.

- *Rhythmics*: Vigorous rhythmic movements are found in great variety these days. Dance, set drills set to music, mass rhythmics, folk dances, aerobics, etc., are universally acknowledged as excellent means of developing dynamic body fitness, sense of rhythm, neuromuscular coordination, body-mind integration, balance, sense of rhythm, and poise in children from a young age.
- *Yoga*: As an Indian traditional system of exercise, and as a philosophy of life, yoga occupies a prestigious position in our physical education. Its benefits to man in terms of improved posture, health, fitness, mental and physical poise, disease prevention, relaxation etc., are difficult to list out. More liberal nations in Europe and else where have started accepting Yoga an important part of their physical education programme.

Physical education is for every one - young, old, man, woman, rich, poor, low and high because health and fitness are the major concerns of every individual today. The scope of physical activity in human education and life is very wide.

NEED AND IMPORTANCE OF PHYSICAL EDUCATION

All organisms live because they move and they move because they live. Movement is the essence of life. For an organism, its purposes are varied.

- It makes the organism reproduce, replicate its genetic material and multiply.

- It enables the organism to *adapt* to the environment and make necessary *adjustments* as and when it is necessary for it to do so for survival.
- Activity motivates the organism to modify its environment, if need be.
- It keeps all vital processes of the organism carried out efficiently.
- It protects the organism from dangers and difficult situations.
- It enables the organism to carry out its struggles for existence.

In man's case, movement does much more than what it does for most other organisms. Besides directing growth and development, movement sharpens man's intellect and intelligence. What man has accomplished through hundreds of millennia of civilization is due to man's ability to perform highly articulated and purposeful movements backed up by a vast repertoire of motor skills acquired through infancy and childhood through formal and informal processes.

Natural movement takes the form of physical exercise - an organized formal way performing certain body movements in certain set sequences for certain specific purposes - when the objective is to maintain an optimal level of development and functional efficiency. Biologically, *use* makes the body organs develop, and *disuse* lets them atrophy. Physical education is an organized physical activity programme that enables participants to maintain quality of life in terms of good health, strength, skill, fitness and vigour.

In these times of speedily increasing inactivity and decreasing movement opportunity even in routines, the need and importance of physical education, as a medium of good health, fitness and recreation has taken precedence over everything else. Regular participation in well-planned and well-conducted physical activity programmes keeps an individual active, alert, fit, and ready to meet various challenges as well as emergencies in life. Daily exercisers are far superior in strength, speed, alertness and work capacity than non-exercisers.

These days, career-conscious students, both at school and college, are over-burdened with academic work which requires sustained concentration resulting in boredom, monotony and mental fatigue. Apart from this, watching television for long hours keeps children indoors and deprived of physical activity. While their nerves are under so much pressure, their muscles remain completely inactive so children lose the ability to live an active life. A physically active short-break between routines of inactivity can possibly remove boredom and sloth, and recharge energy.

It hardly needs emphasis that physical education enables participants to build up reasonable level of fitness – strength, speed, stamina, endurance, agility, flexibility, coordination, etc., – both for life routines and sport. No one can discharge their duties efficiently without adequate fitness. Organic fitness is the primary objective as well as most serious concern of physical education.

Play, recreation, sport and physical activity are an important medium of character building. The historical statement, "Battle of Waterloo was won on the play fields of Eton", speaks volumes about it. Character is a dynamic concept and is developed more readily through active participation in games and sports. Those who do not play, often develop habits and traits of behaviour that are not socially well-appreciated such as fearfulness, cowardice, indecision, timidity, anxiety, etc. Physically *educated* individuals, conversely, are courageous, dominant, confident, and resolute. They can face challenges with firm determination and strong will. Swami Vivekananda had rightly observed: "India needs more of play fields than temples". People strong in body are strong in mind and action; only they are fit to live and protect humanity.

About two thousand five hundred years ago, the Greeks had given a place of pride to physical activity in the system of their education. The Western world has followed this principle in letter and spirit in planning educational experiences for their children. This has served as a basis for their *sports culture* so important for human welfare. The silent killers like stresses, strains, tensions, anxieties, etc., are difficult be tackle without proper education of the body through exercise, play, and sport.

Modern research has shown that the most effective way of disciplining body and mind is to participate in some form of physical activity even for a few minutes on regular basis. Exercising limbs adequately and in a sustained manner is beneficial to the individual and the society physiologically, psychologically and socially. Physical education makes life worth living by canalizing human energies in ingenious ways.

QUESTIONS FOR EXERCISE

Short-answer Questions

On the model of the two solved questions below, answer the questions that follow:

Q.1 : What is education in simple language?

Ans. : Every thing that we do or we are impressed upon to do in a formal or informal way and that which makes us (or our behaviour) better in terms of experience, knowledge, or skill is education. Learning is basic to education and it has no end-line.

Q. 2 : What according to Greek philosophers constituted *complete* education?

Ans. : Socrates, Plato, and Aristotle believed that complete education comprised of aesthetics, ethics, mathematics and athletics (exercise, play, and sports). This contributed very well to the development of a harmonious personality.

1. What distinguishes man from animals?
2. Why is learning known as the basis of education?
3. Write two characteristics of education which shine up human personality.
4. Explain the concept of *sound mind in sound body.*
5. In what way are education and physical education two sides of the same coin?

6. Write an understandable definition of education.
7. List out the major points contained in most definitions of education.
8. In what way is the physical education considered an integral part of education?
9. Define physical education as best as you can.
10. Write five major points of agreement among various definitions of physical education.
11. Briefly describe the aim of physical education.
12. Briefly discuss major objectives of education.
13. What according to National Plan of Physical Education (1956) is the aim of physical education?
14. Define *organic fitness* objectives of physical education.
15. Differentiate between character and personality.
16. What qualities of character do games and sports inculcate in children?
17. Explain the modern concept of modern physical education.
18. What groups of activities fall under the scope of physical education?
19. Write a short note on self-defence activities.
20. Name the types of gymnastics you have seen being practiced and/or performed.
21. Write at least five benefits which people derive from participation physical education programme.
22. How can we discipline our body and mind?
23. What is meant by scope of physical education?
24. Which physical activity has the highest educational value and why?
25. Write a few characteristics of a *physically educated* person.

CHAPTER: TWO

HEALTH EDUCATION & NUTRITION

Herbert Spencer very rightly said: "To be a good animal (fit and healthy) is the first requisite to success in life, and to be a nation of good animals (healthy citizens) is the first condition to national prosperity." This statement points out that health is important for the individual as well as the nation. Without fitness and health, neither an individual nor a nation can sustain for long and be able to achieve the objectives of progress, prosperity and productivity in various fields.

No doubt, most of us are born generally healthy but disease and illness are stark realities of life and it is always our endeavour not to give way to these enemies of life by educating ourselves about diseases, nutrition, exercise, principles and practices of good health. Since ancient times man has always been seriously concerned with his health, fitness and happiness. History of medicine has strong evidence to prove this point. Primitive man attributed suffering, diseases, and natural calamities to the wrath of God and the work of evil spirits. To prevent and rid himself of disease and ill-health, he often prayed to celestial powers, gods and goddesses and indulged in strange rites, rituals, sacrifices and witch craft. As fund of human knowledge increased with experience and research, the perception about disease and ill-health – their causes, remedies, prevention, etc. – began to change, resulting in better understanding of and how to maintain good standards of health and enjoy improved quality of life.

This transformation has come about mainly through the spread of education though the benefits of the modern science of medicine and health have still not reached out to many communities and countries. By and large, there has been tremendous change in the attitude and outlook of man about health, hygiene, exercise, fitness, etc., because it is now well recognized that life without health is a misery, a virtual death and that the real happiness depends not on wealth and riches but on good health, vigour and vitality.

It needs to be understood that improved health and quality of life depend greatly on the improvement of environment, health education and nutrition (balanced diet). The major factor in the entire process is the right kind of education for every one especially the underdog, the unprivileged and the illiterate about diseases, health, nutrition, fitness etc. No stringent laws can do what appropriate education can do to bring about significant change in the health scenario. Therefore, utmost emphasis has to be laid on teaching of principles of health and nutrition in the educational institutions.

MEANING, DEFINITION AND DIMENSIONS OF HEALTH

Health is as wide a concept as life itself; it cannot be defined in a single sentence. Being a quality of life, it must bear a definition that takes cognizance of both positive and negative aspects of it. Health flows from the kind of living that goes on. People do not have health in quantity that can be drawn upon but they have functional powers and abilities that reflect health. How absurd it looks to live badly for eleven months of the year - eating junk food, doing little exercise, taking no preventive measures against disease and indulging in unnecessary and excessive over-eating, drinking, smoking, etc - and expect to restore health in a vacation period as one would deposit money in an exhausted bank account. Other way round, how foolish does it seem to develop strength and vitality in youth but to live unwholesomely and wastefully during the adulthood years. The stream of life will be rich, abundant and lasting in proportion as the sources which nourish it are constantly flowing. Health cannot be assured by thinking good thoughts any more than it can be attained by eating good food while ignoring other considerations. Life is a *whole* and every experience of man contributes its share as well as its effect to make it what it is.

Health is the most valuable possession of man because all life functions receive their vitality from the fountain of health. In *Ayurveda* - the Hindu science of health and longevity - health actually refers to a state of well-balanced metabolism in which body humours perform their functions in immaculate order; it is a happy state of being - a state in which senses and mind are in perfect harmony with the body processes, and vice versa.

Meaning and Definition of Health

For generations, *health* virtually meant *freedom from disease, disability and death*. Now science, research and man's experience have smashed several myths about health and revealed the true nature of human organism with its remarkable possibilities for development, and healthful living beyond the narrow confines of freedom-from-disease. Some people consider "presence of enough energy, vigour and vitality in the body to conduct daily activities", as the essence of health. For others, the basic concept of health is illustrated in the "proper functioning of the various systems of the body".

In Oxford Dictionary, health is defined as "soundness of body or mind: that condition in which its functions are duly and efficiently discharged". In Webster's view, health is "the condition of being sound in body, mind, and spirit, especially freedom from physical disease or pain". A physically *educated* person would be inclined to look at health as "a condition or quality of the human organism in given conditions, genetic and environmental". In the *preamble* to the World Health Organization, health is referred to as "a state of complete physical, mental and social well-being and not merely absence of disease or infirmity". Health is "the quality of life that enables the individual to *live most and cherish best*", stated Jesse Feiring Williams. This concept of health is as broad and as wide as life, because life is more than biological processes of digestion, circulation and elimination, freedom from disease or nutritional habits. Health, as this definition suggests, is capable of enrichment or deterioration; that life at its best is more a realistic concept for all persons than the mere avoidance of disease, and the proper goal of all healthful teaching is the finest kind of individual living.

Maintaining *a perfect* state of health all through life may not be impossible but is certainly difficult as the health-curve affected by several genetic, environmental, personal and social factors and conditions never always moves upwards; it is marked by fluctuations. Aspiring to achieve an optimal level of health so as to live a *personally satisfying* and *socially useful* life, ought to be the major aim of all human endeavours

A few precise definitions of health, as given below, explain the phenomenon of health more elaborately:

> Health is a condition of the organism which measures the degree to which its aggregate powers are liable to function.
>
> ***- Oberteuffer***
>
> Health is considered as that condition, mental and physical, in which the individual is functionally well-adjusted, internally as concerns his body parts, and externally as concerns his environment.
>
> ***- Voltmer and Esslinger***
>
> Health is that state in which the individual is able to mobilize all his resources - intellectual, emotional, and physical, for optimal daily living.
>
> ***- Encyclopaedia of Health***
>
> Health is the condition of being sound in body, mind or spirit, especially freedom from disease or pain.
>
> ***- Webster***

In nutshell, health may be considered as a:

- quality of life, and not simply freedom from disease;
- comprehensive concept covering physical, mental, intellectual, social and cultural aspects of man's daily life;

- realization of man's physical, mental and spiritual powers optimally;
- state in which all functions of the body are duly and efficiently discharged;
- state of well-balanced metabolism; and finally,
- happy state of being.

The ***salient features of the New Philosophy of Health*** are stated as under:

1. Health is fundamental human right; it should not be denied to any one.
2. Health is the essence of productive life, and the result of ever-increasing expenditure on medial care.
3. It is an integral part of human development.
4. It is central to the quality of life.
5. Health is a responsibility of the individual, state, community and the nation - all together.
6. Health, its development and maintenance, is major social investment.
7. It is a worldwide social objective.

People possessing better standards of health and healthful living manifest certain qualities, which those with poor health do not; for example, ability to:

- engage in mental and physical activity
- recover efficiently from the effects of fatigue
- resist fatigue in extraordinary situations
- exhibit increased muscle strength and in certain muscle groups
- make skilled movements; and to incline towards sport
- resist disease and invasion of microbes
- manifest interest and enthusiasm for life
- to be in harmony with the environment and the society
- experience, express and control emotions
- (in the adult) to make and live responsibly

The development of these abilities requires a few biological strengths to begin with, favourable surroundings, and considerable effort on the part of the individual himself.

The role of personal effort in the development of health is very large and significant; it is the individual, not his heredity, nor environment that aspires to attain high levels of vigour, vitality, energy, poise, zeal, zest and kindly understanding. The individual only sets for himself standards of life.

Major Dimensions of Health

Health, today, is a very wide concept and its perceived dimensions go beyond conventional physical, mental and social dimensions. Knowledgeable health educationists consider nutritional, emotional, environmental, preventive, and curative dimensions of health as important as physical and/or social dimensions because changing environment, life-style, attitudes, habits, work requirements, etc., affect human health profoundly, making life an increasingly complex phenomenon. The dimensions of health explained below are interdependent and interactive; they are no isolated concepts.

Physical Dimension

Physical dimension of health takes cognizance of external outlook of the body - its appearance, bearing, complexion, composition, structure, shape, size, the proportion among body parts, etc. The internal aspect of physical dimension of health refers to the functional efficiency of various organic systems of the body. Most of us are born healthy irrespective of our different physical features but disease and ill-health invade us when we do not take care of our body and fail to regulate our nutrition, conduct, behaviour, thinking, emotion, and sleep. We cannot alter our physical dimensions nor can we change our complexion but we can keep healthy, fit and strong by resisting disease, developing healthy tastes and eating habits, engaging in exercise regularly and adequately as well as regulating our work and rest routines. Body is the plinth of our personality and all other accomplishments of life are subordinate to it. Therefore, physical dimension of health is of primary importance and has to be the first focus of attention.

Mental Dimension

Body and mind are an indivisible whole and they provide a necessary integration to human personality. There cannot be physical health without mental health. Mind is the instrument through body moves and accomplishes things. An individual sick in mind is likely to be sick in body. A man is mentally healthy if he carries the least impact of life's stresses, strains and tensions; he thinks good, feels good, lives good, and interacts well with his fellow-beings; such a person is at peace with himself, his environment and with the society at large. In other words, he is well-adjusted and has the capacity to adjust himself according to the changing life situations. Your mind is what you make it and how you programme its software. A person may be as strong as Samson but if he is mentally ill or sick, he is of little worth to humanity; he is just like a dead load on the earth. It is, therefore, imperative that every body must be mentally healthy, have zest and zeal for life and achieve a state of mental equilibrium in which one can "live most and cherish best".

Social Dimension

Man is a social animal, said Aristotle. He is born and brought up in society (family, community, country). He grows and develops by interacting with the social environment which comprises of human beings and their ideas, thoughts, and ideals. Social dimension of health generally refers to man's adjustment in the society, his social relationships, interactions, social learning, etc. Man's biological needs (hunger, thirst, sex, love, etc) and secondary needs (self-respect, competence, recognition, belonging, self-actualization, etc) are satisfied only in society. If there were no society, it would be impossible for man to get humanized as well as socialized and get an identity that characterizes his personality. Recognition to human existence and personality is provided only in society. Apart from being physically fit and strong and mentally sound, one has to be socially well-adjusted. Individual health and social health are close associates. Your being a genius is of little use if you have no healthy relationship with members of your family, your neighbours, your friends, your class-mates, your peers, and your fellow citizens,

Emotional Dimension

Emotions are intense feelings having psycho-physiological implications in human behaviour. They are contagious too. Love, aggression, anger, fear, disgust, depression, frustration, anxiety, etc., are all emotions. It is said that our deepest feelings (emotions) along with our passions and longings are essential guides to our character and personality and they play a very significant role in all human affairs. They influence our reasoning and our decision-making ability at crucial moments. Under the influence of emotions (high arousal) we often do things which we would not if we were normal and rational. Several situations, in our daily life, arouse our emotions and spoil the prospectus of deciding things in a right way. A healthy person must also be emotionally controlled, a thought so difficult to realize. Positive emotions (love, laughter, affection) sustain good health, negative ones (anger, fear, anxiety) ruin it by leaving a residual effect on the organism causing psychosomatic diseases. Many people are today suffering from cardiac disorders because they are not emotionally balanced. Health without emotional equilibrium is worth pittance.

Spiritual Dimension

Man is a trio of body, mind and spirit. While body and mind are well represented in the conventional concept of health, spiritual dimension is a new addition and still not very well highlighted. There is something beyond body and mind that impacts and directs human growth, development, behaviour and conduct. It is the divine side of our existence. This also needs proper care and feeding. Surely, it raises man from the animal state to that of godliness. Health is incomplete without spiritual uplift, understanding and awakening. If one wanted to be healthy and happy, one must have some spiritual accomplishment that leads to some contentment.

Nutritional Dimension

Besides air and water, food is the very basis of our existence. Nutrition plays an extremely important role in the maintenance of health. Under-fed and ill-fed people live a life of worms, insects and beasts, perhaps worse. People with poor nutritional status suffer from variety of diseases of body and mind. Malnutrition is a big hindrance in the proper growth of body and mind. Human productivity is badly affected when people possess no requisite strength, and lack sustaining power at work. Nutritional imbalance seriously affects child bearing and child rearing. The health of a nation has to bear various onslaughts due to malnutrition. As an important component of health, nutrition must attract due attention of the individual and nation at large.

Preventive and Curative Dimension

Malnutrition, illhealth and disease are hard facts of life and must be tackled by preventive and curative measures. Prevention is far better than cure and the habit of preventing diseases, mishaps and accidents (which ruin one's health) is formed by proper education and engaging in right kind of health practices. In the maintenance of health, principles of prevention play a very critical role and good education must lay emphasis on their teaching right from the beginning. Once disorder or disease has occurred, it requires cure and people must learn how to take care of simple ailments and go for right medical aid in case of complex health problems. Proper sanitation, hygiene, cleanliness, etc., are important measures against disease and illhealth.

Environmental Dimension

The two major health-influencing factors are heredity and environment. While we have *no* control over our genetics; we have enough power with us to control environmental factors that pose a serious threat to human health such as insanitation, pollution, malnutrition, accidents, social hazards like drinking, smoking, alcohol, etc. When people learn to keep their surroundings clean and ensure a pollution-free environment, many rather most health problems pertaining to health can be solved without much spending whether by the State or other agencies. The wise consumption of natural resources like wood, water, coal, air, etc., goes a long way in improving health of people in general.

HEALTH EDUCATION

Among all kinds of education that we have in schools, colleges, universities and other centres of higher learning, health education definitely occupies a place of pride because without good health, man can perform no functions of life – physical and mental. For many people, health education is an abstract concept. This is not a true assessment of health education either because the principles and practices that fall within the purview of health education are so clear, understandable and practicable, e.g. balanced, diet, its resources, its composition, its elements and its preparation; need for air, water, ventilation, proper temperature, rest and sleep; personal hygiene, (habits of cleanliness wit regard to body), dress, dwelling; knowledge of the structure of the body, its systems, organs and their functions as they affect health; common diseases, their causes, symptoms, their prevention and the curative measures; sanitation at home, school, work-place, villages, towns; health care, etc.

The major aim of health education is to acquaint people, in general, with the principles and practices of health maintenance, apprise them of evil consequences of bad health habits and hazards and inculcate in them healthy habits of consuming nutritious food, making the environment pollution free, observing personal hygiene and engaging in some form of physical activity, play, games and sports.

Definition of Health Education

In common language, the medium or means that are

capable of informing and educating an individual in matters of his health and the mechanics of its maintenance falls within the purview of health education - whether at school or outside it. People acquire knowledge about diseases, health practices, about ways and means to improve the standard of their health etc., by observation, self-experience and/or by formal instruction at school. This and much more constitutes health education. Keeping health education at par with general education, the World Health Organization explicitly states that it (health education) is "concerned with changes in knowledge, feelings and behaviour of people. In most usual forms, health education concentrates on developing such health practices as are believed to bring about the best possible state of well-being." It is a part and parcel of general education as well as physical education, making it incumbent upon the educational administration to recognize its need at all levels of education. For proper maintenance of students' health at school or at college and at home as well as to inculcate in pupils the life-long healthy habits, health education must precede any other type of education.

Health education is a universal education; it is for the young and the old, for men and women, for the rich and the poor, for the low and the high, and the backward and the forward because health must, first of all, has to be the primary concern of every individual and every nation. If one wished to live a healthy, active and vibrant life, one must educate oneself in the ways of good health both by precept and practice.

While the general health education derives its content from (1) human biology,(2) nutrition, (3) hygiene - personal and environmental, (4) family health care, (5) control of communicable diseases, (6) mental health, (7) prevention of accidents, and (8) use of health services, a school health education programme specifically addresses general cleanliness, ventilation, health examination, health instruction, water supply (pure and unpolluted), exercise and sports, inculcation of healthy habits in children, and a good civic sense, both in theory and in practice.

There is no two opinion about the fact that health education is primarily related to efforts one makes to truly educate himself in all crucial matters and aspects of health. It hardly matters whether such education comes through formal means e.g. school teaching or informal means like observation and casual interaction with varied people - members of the family, peer group on the playfield, elders and significant individuals at the club or at social meetings.

With such a vast canvas and scope, health education is difficult to describe and explain. Yet as an academic exercise, an effort has to be made to explain its purpose, focus, objective and function. Like health, health education has a variety of meanings and its usage differs from person to person and from one context to another. Caring mothers and elementary schools teachers informally teach small kids how to brush teeth, to comb hair, to take bath and to develop good habits of eating, drinking, wearing clothes, etc. Doctors, physicians, nurses and other paramedical personnel have to train themselves formally to keep people healthy by applying principles of health through an organized effort. A business executive may simply like to know how to sharpen his appetite, while a health-conscious adult may read quite a lot about health. People differ in their concept of health education and their attitude towards it. Today health education has become an organized academic discipline and a field of professional practice.

Health education is that phase of life-experience in which a person *educates* himself about health - its development, and maintenance - in its holistic form in order to ensure his wellbeing through out life. It is a life-long process, and virtually commences with the mother teaching her baby regular 'potty' habits, and continues with the child being taught the regular and adequate sleeping, eating and drinking habits. All these healthy habits learnt in early childhood help to build strong bodies, which remain healthy in later life. When children are small their parents take care of their health and educate them but as they grow up, they learn and practice more about health either through self-experience or formal lessons at school.

Health education may mean many things to many people, but its definition adopted by the National Conference on the Preventive Medicine in the United States has a universal acceptance:

> Health education is a process that informs, motivates and helps people to adopt and maintain healthy practices and life-styles, advocates environmental changes as needed to facilitate this goal, and conducts professional training and research to the same end.

A few more definitions of health education given below preset an interesting scenario about this important discipline.

> Health education is a process that bridges the gap between health information and health practices. Health education motivates the person to take the information and do something with it, to keep himself healthier, by avoiding actions that are harmful, and practicing those that are beneficial.
>
> ***- US President's Committee on Health Education***
>
> Health education aims at creating such a quality of life as may enable an individual to live most and serve best.
>
> ***- World Health Organization Expert Committee***
>
> Health education is the sum experiences which favourably influence habits, attitudes and knowledge, relating to individual, community and social health.
>
> ***- Dr. Thomas Wood***
>
> Health education is concerned with the health related behaviour of people.
>
> ***- Sophie***
>
> Health education is a systemic programme for developing healthy habits, attitudes and knowledge that will contribute to physical, mental and emotional healths.
>
> ***- Unknown***

In nutshell, health education is:

- a part of general education and physical education;
- knowledge of principles of maintaining health;
- information on health hazards, diseases, their prevention, and cure;
- a process that brings about changes in man's attitudes, knowledge, behaviour and feeling about themselves, their health and their life;
- concerned with health-related behaviours and practices; and

- for every one without any distinction of caste, age, creed, language, or race.

Objectives of Health Education

A general consensus points out that the *major objective* of health education is to bridge the gap between scientific knowledge of functioning of the human body and maintenance of health and practical application of the principles personal hygiene, exercise, sleep, rest etc. However, Ruth Grout has enumerated the following four objectives of health education:

1. Optimum development of the individual with special reference to physical and emotional development.
2. Betterment of human relationships, particularly from the standpoint of health.
3. Application of facts and principles in respect of economic efficiency in the production and consumption of goods and services.
4. Civic responsibility, especially in respect to health

Development of knowledge of or informing people about health, development of desirable health attitude, and development of desirable health practices have also been quoted as important objectives of health education.

Inherent in the comprehensive definition of health education adopted by the National Conference on Preventive Medicine in USA, are three ***major objectives***:

(1) To spread awareness among people about the methods and means of prevention of disease and promotion of health;

(2) To motivate people to practice principles of health and develop healthy habits among them; and

(3) To press into service the health academia to conduct professional training and research so as to achieve the goals of health education.

Under first objective, people are expected to acquire knowledge, both through self-effort and structured instruction at school, about maxims and principles of health; causes, cures and preventive measures of various diseases; health-promoting factors; and general human anatomy and physiology. In adulthood and old age, knowledge about health comes by reading good literature on the subject and watching health programmes on the television. Many people are no doubt knowledgeable about health, but they possess not many healthy habits. They drink, smoke, over eat, hardly engage in any physical exercise and are often irregular in their toilet habits. They are fully aware that what they do will ultimately lead to illhealth and yet, by force of habit, sloth or devil-may-care attitude, they remain indifferent to the ill effects of their unhealthy habits and behaviours.

Under second objective, health education must provide such learning experiences to the people as favourably influence their life-styles, habits, attitudes and ethics relating to their own health, and that of others around them. It must act as a motivating force to help people discard habits and behaviours that are detrimental to health and adopt those that promote health.

Research and training, which constitute ***the third objective*** of health education, expand the horizons of knowledge about health in all its dimensions and keep people abreast of the latest techniques of fighting the menace of diseases, environmental hazards, pollution, and ecological degradation and how to check it. The health authorities, in hospitals, medical colleges, or in the local self-government level must voluntarily take up this responsibility. People need to be educated and trained in tackling health problems at home and at public places as and when required, and not always look to government for assistance and action.

In ***school setting,*** health education addresses incidentally three major objectives, more or less similar in nature to those explained above: (a) health instruction, (b) health supervision, and (c) health environment.

Health instruction refers to that aspect of formal teaching-learning process through which the students are instructed in basic principles of health generally covering knowledge about common diseases, their causes, remedial and preventive aspects; personal hygiene; body-care; first aid; correct postures of sleeping, sitting, standing, walking, running etc. Health instruction falls within the purview of the physical education at school.

Health supervision is sometimes interpreted to mean school providing health services, within the affordable limits. Under this functional objective, every student must be subjected to a health examination at least once a year and their medical records maintained properly under the supervision of the physical education teacher. The school should engage a medical officer on regular or part basis to do this job and prescribe remedial for the students suffering from ill-health and disease.

Health environment constitutes all external factors that affect a student's health especially at school such as class rooms, playfields, surroundings, footpaths, cycle stands, stair cases, various fixtures (electrical fitting, play areas, open-air gyms, slides, swings, etc.), drinking water, games and sports, and so on. Under the health education programme, the school must make sure that standards of health are maintained while providing and maintaining such facilities. Objects and services that pose potential danger to health of a child at school must immediately be removed. Children learn by and large greatly by observation (imitation) for which a healthy environment at school is necessary.

Importance of Health Education

Until the advent of the *Age of Science*, ill-health, disease, and death were considered as national calamities. Most people attributed their occurrence to forces of nature or even providence. Today, even a school-going child knows pretty well how most diseases are caused and how they can be cured; how it is important to follow simple but significant principles of health and how injuries and accidents can be prevented by following certain guidelines of conduct and behaviour. This is all on account of the essential knowledge being imparted to children in health, hygiene, personal and environmental cleanliness, human body and its functioning, etc., through formal teaching and electronic media.

The unprecedented advancements in medicine, health sciences and technology have helped man to narrow the gap between ignorance and knowledge to a great extent about human wellbeing and reduce the risks and dangers arising from disease and environmental hazards. By way of education, through self-experience, literature study and electronic media, people receive instruction in the causes, cure and prevention of diseases, anatomy and physiology, fitness, exercise, health, hygiene and related subjects so that every one gets due opportunity to keep healthy, fit and strong. Health education intelligently strikes at the root of ignorance, misconceptions, prides and prejudices so widely spread among people about health and health practices. It makes people aware of their health needs, problems, obstacles in the way of achieving the requisite health standards and the responsibilities they need to discharge in ensuring individual, family, societal and environmental health.

Health education is a strong motivating force for people of all shades to have a critical look at their lifestyle and make efforts to change all those habits and behaviours that impinge upon one's health and endanger life. Nothing worthwhile can be achieved in the area of individual, community and national health until and unless people get inspired to take care of their surroundings and environment and go all out to eradicate factors and check forces, detrimental to human health such as contamination of water and beverages, pollution of all sorts, open-air defaecation, consumption of alcohol, drug addiction, smoking, physical inactivity, and so on. In health and personal hygiene matters persuasion, and motivation work wonders, not coercion or compulsion. For example, when *family planning* drive was launched in the country in 70s with over-spilling enthusiasm to the brink of coercion, almost every one literally revolted against it. On the other hand, encouraging effects of education, inspiration and persuasion about this could best be seen almost every where especially in the states like Kerala. Health by motivation and not by compulsion is the core of modern health education.

The worth of health education lies in its ability to provide *learning-by-doing* experience for all to ensure a substantial positive transformation in their thinking, attitude, mindset, and outlook about the health needs and health problems of the individual, family, community, and the country as a whole. The health education programme, for all settings and individuals, should be all-absorbing and all-involving. It ought to be attractive in the sense that it should put responsibility on every one irrespective their position, status and placement in the social fabric. It should be educative in its objective. People ask for precise but handy information and guidance on balanced diet, healthy habits, health practices, child care, cooking, serving food, eating habits, etc. They must get it freely with frequent reminders. Education in nutrition is a major strategy in preserving and maintaining health. Malnutrition is a curse on millions and a crime against humanity; only proper education can eliminate it.

Without health education, it is impossible to improve one's social and economic standard. Much of the poverty and backwardness in our country are due to absence of proper education about personal hygiene and cleanliness especially in villages and among women. This keeps them socially and economically backward. A healthy person is an asset to his family, his community and to the country, because he is strong and productive. By and large, he lives happily. An unhealthy individual is a curse on himself and a liability on others; he only demands – attention, care, medicine, help, time, and so on. Proper education about health can change this dark scenario considerably.

Health of the people is a civic and public responsibility. Therefore, both the local administration and the state government are obliged to provide necessary infrastructure for health services and also organize health training programmes for the common people in order to help them carry the message to the grass-root level, in the town or the village. Family Planning Campaign, National Malaria Eradicating Programme, Polio-vaccination Campaign, Tuberculosis Control Programme, etc., have had a salutary effect on the health-improving efforts of the people. These ventures have also been a great source of education for every one through visual and media publicity. The aim of giving some place to health education in the school curricula is to:

- create health-awareness among children
- instill healthy habits among children right from the very beginning
- make students participants in national development programme
- use student-power in keeping the environment pollution-free
- make children an instrument of health education for adults and the backward
- eradicate religious and social taboos about health through educational process
- bring radical change in the attitudes and habits of the people through student public relation programme.

Health education has to be accepted as the starting point of all education all human endeavours, invariably, depend on good health. Human suffering can be considerably reduced if health education is imparted to every one right from the impressionable age. It is just not possible to bring down the rate of child mortality, cut down on the number of accidents on the road, at home, at work place and in the school, control communicable diseases, prevent health hazards, check incidence of psycho-somatic disorders, and provide assured well-being to all without health education being imparted in schools, clubs, in the media, and other public places. In the matter of human health, only education is the key to success.

Principles of Health Education

Children learn by observation, self-effort and by formal teaching process in a classroom. Different areas of knowledge and activities are learnt by different methods. Like motor skills and sport & athletic skills require first mental absorption of technique, followed by physical practice to perfection; principles of health education are assimilated through observation and instruction, at home, at school and at public places. Healthy habits are learnt and repeated over time to become a part of behaviour. Therefore, inspiration, motivation and practice are significant processes of inculcating healthy habits in an individual through various developmental stages. Effective results may be obtained by creating an atmosphere in which people get used to assimilating, right from childhood, significant ideas about health and developing such healthy attitudes, habits and modes of behaviour as are highly conducive to maintaining good health through out life. This is the crux of health education.

Important principles of health education may be enumerated as under:-

1. No health effort is likely to meet with reasonable success unless people realize the worth of that effort and give it a *whole-hearted support*. We often do things better in which we are interested. Therefore, interest is a big motivating force, which are developed in an individual or group by persuasion, inspiration, and persistence. Slogans like "Be Fit" or "Keep Healthy" or "Run for Health" sound hollow, when people do not follow their spirit and act accordingly. People ought to be kept motivated all the time to take care of their health.
2. Necessity is the mother of invention is a well-known maxim. We hardly do any thing unless there is a *felt-need* to do so. Let health and health education, focus on the need of the hour. A need-based health education shall have ready acceptance and voluntary following. It needs to be noted that all are not conscious

of their health problems and needs, nor all have access to remedial measures. In fact, people need be woken up to their health needs. Slum dwellers and those living in congested areas have different health needs than those living in posh colonies.

3. As in general education, so in health education, following *principle of progression,* proceed from known to unknown, concrete to abstract and simple to complex. Start with what people already know and gradually introduce what they need to know, thereby making health education a systematic process. Let people understand things and practice them as they get aware about them. Every idea should be within intellectual grasp of the people. Success comes quickly as we begin with the known and gradually inch towards what is unknown. Unrelated and unknown facts do not get easily assimilated.
4. Use the *communication media* – especially language – that best suit people. Unfamiliar and difficult-to-follow language makes a mess of the learning situation. Simple principles of science or health should be explained in simple, understandable and easy-to-grasp language – possibly local dialect. The use of vernacular fetches good response and better results in terms of learning.
5. Health effort should be *reinforced* and followed up until it leads to success. Health education symbolizes principles that require constant practice. In order to instill healthy habits among infants and children, both parents and teachers must see that children observe standards of regularity and punctuality in their personal hygiene (for example, they brush their teeth at least twice a day, take bath, comb hair, etc). A regular inspection on children's habits of eating, drinking, sleeping, playing, etc., is a must. Constant reminder, in theory and practice, is necessary in cultivating good habits. Behaviours are reinforced by frequent reminders and repetition of acts.

6. Health is a basis for survival; it is a requirement for work-efficiency and productivity. Without proper *understanding of its principles and processes*, no health standards can be maintained. Motivation for health knowledge, awareness and education must come from primary sources (biological needs, drives, and motives), and secondary reinforcements (praise, blame, social approval, reward, punishments, etc.). Let every one, without exception, realize the worth and value of being healthy and fit and the role health education plays in his/her efforts to get educated in this regard. Monetary benefits and incentives are temporary measures of temporary change in human behaviour; they should be discreetly used.
7. In the matter of health and education, nothing succeeds more than *learning-by-doing*. Healthy habits have to be practiced in order to be learnt. A Chinese proverb illustrates this point wonderfully: "If I hear, I forget; if I see, I remember; if I do, I know". Practicing means knowing and knowing leads to doing. No blackboard operation can impart any practical knowledge about health. Only with participation and practice can people acquire health and healthy habits.
8. Both health education and health practices must draw their substance from the *scientific facts*, not hearsay, witchcraft, tradition or quackery. Science and tradition are opposed to each other, but science has with it light of the truth; it should not be sacrificed for tradition.
9. Make health education media *attractive, viable and palatable*. Often the subjects (people) are compared to the soil, health facts (knowledge, education) to seeds, and transmitting media (ways, means, methods, techniques) to the sower. The relationship among all the three is complete and unquestionable. Good thoughts and good acts must have good transmission media.

10. Health education without *human relationship* is a body without soul. That human relationship is at the heart of all education needs no elaboration. The health-educator must act as a friend, philosopher and guide to all he comes in contact with.
11. Health education without *competent leadership* is like a headless horseman who knows no direction. A headman in a village, a teacher at school and a social worker in society play a key role in educating people about health. A leader has authority over his followers by virtue of being a man of conviction and character. His word is an order for others. Community leadership and health leadership must work in close proximity and cooperation.
12. Health education is a *cooperative affair* and all agencies – school, college, the municipal corporation, state and central governments – must make a coordinated effort to educate people in the matters of health and hygiene. There has to be a concerted effort to this effect in order to achieve better results.
13. Health education is *no one time job*; it is an ongoing activity and must be continued unhindered without any break. The problem of health appears in different garb and at different times without any fore-warning. It is necessary to take both short-term and long-term measures to educate people and improve their health.
14. Health educators and physical educators must *work hand-in-hand* to raise the standard of health of the school children since physical activity is an important ingredient of health education programme. Without physical activity in adequate measure, health education programme may not bear good fruit.

BALANCED DIET, ITS ELEMENTS AND SOURCES

The effort to secure food characterizes man's basic drives. All our energy, whether manifested in growth and development of the body and mind or the activities we perform, comes from the food that we eat. The chemical compounds in food, delivered to every cell of the body after the complex processes of digestion, absorption, and assimilation, enable our life activities to go on. Our vital processes of life - the organic ones that maintain the organism, the growth of the young into the adult, good and noble thoughts and/or the bad behavioral designs - all flow from the energies made available to us by the chemical compounds of the food.

Food performs following functions in our body:

1. It builds up or renews tissues as a result of which, we grow structurally and functionally, and improve upon our physical and mental dimensions.
2. The ingested food yields energy in the form of heat units for action. Our working efficiency greatly increases with the nutritious food we eat.
3. Food regulates body processes and stimulates cell functions such as maintaining body temperature. Several elements of food perform this function.

Nutrition is a science which deals with human food and how our body utilizes it.

Importance of Nutrition

Eating right kind of food containing important constituents in right proportion to sustain ourselves as well as to carry on various activities efficiently is important. The problems of food and nutrition are very acute through out the world. Some people are over-fed; others are under-nourished. Both suffer in their characteristic ways and face health problems. The problem of nutrition, in general, is largely due to poverty and lack of proper education. Scientists have discovered variety of facts concerning human nutrition, but only a small number of people apply them in the process of what to eat and how to eat.

The economically backward, i.e. poor people have no access to nutritious food. Their problem is largely economic. Contrarily, the rich have the ability to buy wholesome foods but their preferences are poor. They have wrong eating habits. Their problem is mainly educational. The way housewives manage their kitchen and the cooks cook, goes a long way in developing eating habits in most people.

In the matter of nutrition, the three considerations of paramount importance are; (1) in life, nutritious food should be the first priority because health largely depends on this; (2) every one must select right preferences for food and develop good eating habits; (3) whatever one eats, it must be cooked properly.

Our notions of normal nutrition have undergone a sea change during the recent years. With an average nutrition, it is possible just to live but with an optimal dietary man may grow larger and stronger, and possibly lives longer. It is well known that physique is conditioned by diet and that latent growth potential powers are not fully realized in the absence of balanced diet. Generally, dietary deficiencies in vitamin D and calcium, for instance, are quite frequent even among quite affluent people and these lacks are responsible for the growth lags and dental caries.

Victims of either under-nutrition or malnutrition have children with stunted growth and afflicted with several diseases. Such children show no interest in studies and remain backward through out life. Anemia, rickets, postural deformities, ill-formed bones, susceptibility to diseases, etc., result from nutritional deficiencies.,The diet, fitness and health are inter-related concepts. It is experimentally established that no healthy state of body and mind can be maintained without good nutrition and healthy eating habits. It is wisely said, "*animals feed, man eats*. Only the man of intellect and judgment knows (what to eat and) how to eat".

Functions of Food in the Body and Meaning of a Balanced Diet

As a basic principle of life, ***we do not live to eat; we eat to live*** - not only to live but to live to perform various activities and to achieve various objective of life. When we entered this world, eating came to us naturally and instinctively. In the beginning, we ate whatever was offered to us by our caring parents, nurses, or cooks and gradually as we advanced in years, we learnt to eat according to what pleased us and also how to eat using our experience as well as directed by formal instruction at school or else where. Human body is a very complex organism which sustains itself when air, water and food are made available to it in appropriate amount to meet the needs of the body in relation to the circumstances provided all environmental factors and forces influencing the organism remain favourable.

It is one thing to eat what is readily available in order to survive, but quite another to have rich, abundant, varied and perennial supply of food that caters to our bodily requirement in order to live vigorously, abundantly and productively. It needs no reminder that human body is not a simple structure of bones, muscles, nerves, lymph, etc; it is a thinking and performing machine that interacts with the environment by generating its own propulsive energy out of the food it consumes. In order for each and every cell of the body to get regular supply of required energy, man must eat food that it is rich in chemicals, necessary for producing power in the organism to survive and function at an optimal level of physical and mental efficiency. The chemicals present in the food that human body needs, are called ***nutrients***.

Nutritionists attribute the following functions to the food in our body:

1. Food yields energy to various organs of the body to perform their functions as efficiently as possible.
2. It builds up tissues, enabling new ones to grow and replace those worn out through use.
3. Food provides chemicals that regulate and stimulate body processes that control our growth and development, and facilitate protection from diseases.
4. Food also provides us psychological satisfaction. It is an important means of developing social relationships too.

Somewhere in an Upanishad it is said: 'human body is all food; from food it rises and at the end, food it becomes for other organisms'.

Balanced Diet

The food that we eat must be *perfect* and a perfect food, in real sense of the term, is one that contains all the basic elements (or constituents) - carbohydrates, proteins, fats, vitamins, minerals, salts, water etc. - in adequate proportions necessary for the body to grow and function at its optimal efficiency. In other words, ***a balanced diet*** comprises of appropriate types and in adequate measures of foods and drinks that provide nutrition and energy to the body for the growth, maintenance, replacement and functioning of the cells, tissues, organs and organ-systems and to assist the normal development of the individual.

Foods vary widely in their chemical composition, and also in service they give to the body economy. It would, therefore, be impossible for a few items of food to supply all the nutrients needed for the body. In the light of this fact, a balanced diet must contain the proper amount of each nutrient that may come from a variety of sources and food stuffs.

A ***good (balanced) diet*** must contain all the essential ingredients of food (nutrition) in appropriate proportion i.e. carbohydrates (sugar, sweets, bakery products) 57%, fats (oils, dairy products) 30%, proteins (eggs), milk, meat, poultry, fish etc) 13%, vitamins, minerals, salts, water etc., in adequate amount. No doubt our diet varies from one season to another the proportion of various nutrients remains almost constant varying only with the nature and intensity of the physical activities and mental tasks we engage in. For instance, when we do some form of manual work or play a vigorous sport (athletics, swimming, football or up-the-hill running), our intake of food correspondingly shoots up; we need more of carbohydrates and fats as fuel for the body. On the other hand, when we take in more calories than we burn, we put on weight and become vulnerable to a variety of diseases. It needs to be noted that our age, sex, body surface, duration and intensity of the physical activity we engage in, our emotional states, our eating habits, customs and traditions, climatic conditions, our genetic make-up relating to our growth and health etc., influence the quantity and quality of our diet. Our basic requirement for food and enhanced requirement in relation to the higher demands put on our body too are subject to fluctuation due to several known and unknown factors and conditions - both personal and environmental.

A ***wholesome daily diet*** must look-like the one recommended below:

Milk	1 pint (one quart for children)
Egg	1 daily (on days not used, substitute more milk, cheese. Peanuts, meat or other protein food)
Meat, Fowl or Fish	1 or more servings
Potato	1 or more
Vegetables	2 or more servings; one green or yellow
Fruits	2 or more; one citrus fruit or tomato or other food source of vitamin c
Cereals and Bread	Whole-grain or enriched

Sweets, fats, starchy and other foods should be added to complete the meals and to maintain normal weight.

Elements or (Constituents) and their Sources

Food, in general, contains a large variety of nutrients but food scientists have grouped them into six main classes - carbohydrates, proteins, fats, vitamins, minerals & salts, and water. On the basis of their functionality, they have been classified into three categories: (a) those that yield energy, (b) those that build tissue, and (c) those that regulate and stimulate body processes. They are discussed below in the same order.

Energy-Yielding Foods

Carbohydrates and fats are the major source of energy. They are oxidized in the body to produce bio-energy i.e. ATP. So they are called biological fuels of the body. Energy is needed in the body to make certain substance such as glycogen, proteins, etc., move muscles and bones, and to accomplish certain other functions.

Carbohydrates

Carbohydrates are the most abundant and most economical sources of energy. They are a class of chemical compounds composed of carbon, hydrogen and oxygen; and are found in monosaccharide, disaccharide and polysaccharide groups. Sugars, starch and glucose are carbohydrates, as also is cellulose, which forms the bulk of the undigested roughage in human food. While starch has no taste and is insoluble in water, glucose is the simplest form of carbohydrate and is the *instant* source of energy. The cooked starch gets easily and completely digested into glucose. As reserve carbohydrate, glucose is stored in the body - in greatest quantity in the liver and muscles - in the form of glycogen. Unlike starch grains, glycogen dissolves in water and is readily broken down by appropriate enzymes to yield glucose. Complete combustion of 1 gram of carbohydrate (glucose) in the body yields 4.2 kilocalories of energy.[1 (one) calorie is the amount of heat required to raise the temperature of 1 (one) gram of water by 1%.] The basis energy requirement of man every hour is 1.3 calories per kilogram of body-weight. Training athletes may require 8.5 calories per kg of weight per hour. Excess carbohydrates get converted into fat by the liver and stored in the adipose tissue.

Some meat-eating tribes are known to get little or no carbohydrate in their diet and yet stay alive and healthy. Nevertheless from necessity most men are at least partial vegetarians and carbohydrate is the chief component of their diet.

Main sources of Carbohydrates are wheat, maize, rice, bajra, potato, sweet potato, corn, tapioca, banana, sugar, sugar cane, many ripe fruits, etc. Candies, Indian sweets, chocolates etc. are also rich in carbohydrates but too much of their consumption creates some acute problems of health.

Fats

Chemically known as ***lipids***, fats are heterogeneous group of organic compounds containing glycerol and fatty acids. They may be divided into (a) *simple lipids* (oils, fats, and waxes), and (b) *compound lipids* (phospholipids, glycolipids, and sterols). Like carbohydrates, fats are also made up of carbon, hydrogen and oxygen atoms. The major difference between the two constituents of food is that the fats contain less proportion of oxygen than carbohydrates. The word *fat*, when used in anatomical sense, refers to adipose tissue. In chemical sense, fats are glyceryl esters of fatty acids. They are hydrolyzed to yield three molecules of fatty acid and one molecule of glycerol.

Some fats like ghee, butter, vanaspati, etc., are called *saturated fats* as they remain solid at room temperature; *unsaturated fats* like groundnut oil, linseed oil, cotton-seed oil, olive oil, etc., remain in liquid form at room temperature. This is important from the medical point of view especially metabolic utilization of the fat in the body.

Fats are the richest source of energy of our body. When completely combusted, one gram of fat releases 9.3 kcal which is 2.25 times more than the energy given out by one gram of glucose. Serving as energy-reserve, fats are stored in the liver, bones, muscles, adipose tissue, under the skin and around kidneys, and heart to be used as energy after oxidation when glucose is not available. Fats play an important role in the formation of certain steroid hormones, e.g. testosterone, aldosterone, etc. They help in absorption of food, serve as a shock-absorbing cushion to eyeballs, kidneys, ovaries etc., and act as insulator for the nerve fibres and the body against heat loss. Fats add taste to the food and also protect hair.

The ***chief sources of animal fat*** are milk, cheese, butter, purified butter (*ghee*), egg-yolk, meat, oily fish, etc. The vegetable fats are richly derived from various types of nuts such as walnut, almond, groundnut, coconut, etc. Mustard seed, sesame seed, sunflower seed, soybean, maize, olive fruit, etc. also contain a lot of fats.

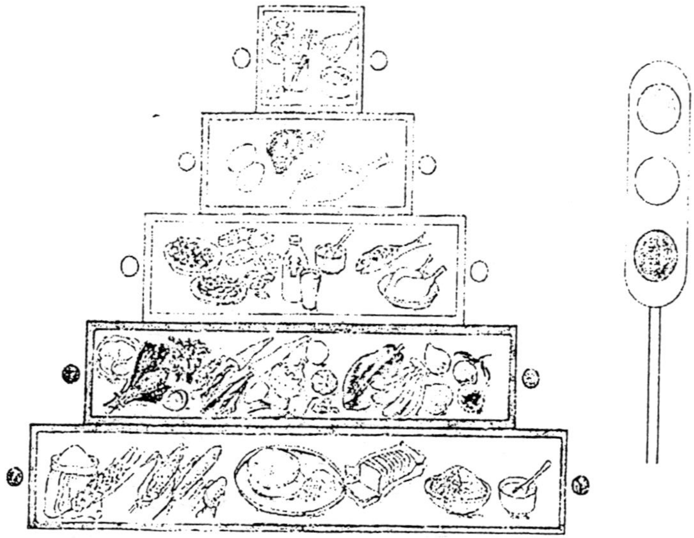

Fig. 2.1 The body-building foods

Body-building Foods

The human body needs energy to perform various activities. It also requires material to build up its structure as well as to sustain it, and repair the tissues that are subject to constant wear and tear. Since the proteins serve these ends, they are truly called the building blocks of the body.

Proteins

Considered as the basic structural material of the body, proteins are more complex than either carbohydrates or fats and they differ from them in containing *nitrogen* besides the carbon, hydrogen, and oxygen, which all the three contain. Sometimes, sulfur, phosphorus or iron may also be found in them. Proteins are built up of simpler substances called *amino acids* that contain amino group instead of hydrogen.

In our body, proteins perform the following functions characteristic of them:

(1) They act as catalyst for the digestion of food. Amylase, lipase, pepsin, trypsin, etc., are all enzyme proteins.

(2) The hormone proteins like insulin secreted by pancreas regulate blood sugar.

(3) The transport proteins such as haemoglobin carry oxygen to cells and transport back carbon dioxide.

(4) The contractile proteins like myosin and actin help the muscles to contract.

(5) The function of the structural proteins is to form the structural elements of the cells and tissues of the body.

(6) The protective proteins such as gamma globulins present in the blood act as antibodies to help fight infection.

Proteins are essential for physical and mental growth, and functioning of the body. Their deficiency causes several diseases. Proteins vary in their constituents and their nutritive value, depending upon their amino acid composition. As a result they are categorized as *adequate* and *inadequate* proteins. The adequate proteins contain all the amino acids for the growth and maintenance of the body, where as inadequate proteins furnish material for energy needs only. In general, the proteins of animal origin most nearly meet the essential needs of the body.

The best plant ***sources of proteins*** are groundnuts, cashew nuts, almonds, chestnuts, beans, peas, and whole cereals such as wheat, maize and pulses. The animal proteins are obtained from the lean meat (meat without fat) of goat, sheep, deer, chicken; and fish, egg, milk, cheese and curd.

Protective Foods

Vitamins and minerals are known as protective foods. Their absence in the body causes "deficiency diseases". Numerous anatomical and physiological functions of the body get setback if their supply is hampered.

Vitamins

The vitamins are organic substances, which the body needs, in small quantities for its normal metabolism and growth. They may not provide energy as carbohydrates or fats do, nor do they serve as building materials as proteins or mineral do but are considered essential for all cells. Though needed in the diet in minute amounts, minerals nevertheless are responsible for catalyzing certain chemical reactions, maintaining good health and ensuring normal growth of the body. Vitamins are a group of fifteen substances, unrelated to each other in their chemical structure. They are mostly synthesized by plants and bacteria and supplied by diet. The human body synthesizes only vitamins D and K. Each vitamin occurs in a particular kind of food and each one performs a specific function. A balanced diet must essentially contain all kinds of vitamins in required quantity.

Some vitamins such as vitamin B complex and vitamin C are water-soluble, where as vitamins A, D, E, and K are fat-soluble. The water-soluble vitamins are absorbed along with water in gastrointestinal tract and remain dissolved in the body fluids. The body stores no vitamins; if found in excess quantity, they are excreted in the urine. The fat-soluble vitamins are absorbed with ingested dietary fats by the small intestine and can be stored in liver cells and adipose tissues.

Vitamin A is necessary for maintaining healthy eyesight and normal epithelia of skin and hair. Green and leafy vegetables (carrot, spinach) and fruits (papaya, ripe mango), maize, egg-yolk, whole milk, butter, *ghee*, cod fish-liver oil, shark-liver oil and liver contain it abundantly. Vitamin A is stored in the liver in large quantity. Strong light destroys it.

Vitamin B complex is known to consist of eight different components, of which the following five are extremely important:

> *Vitamin B_1* is essential for growth, aerobic carbohydrate metabolism, functioning of heart, nerves and muscles. It is present in yeast extract, rice or wheat germ (whole grain cereals),

groundnuts, beans, soybean, liver, pulses, lean meat, milk, sea food, green vegetables, etc. Over-cooking and backing of the food containing it destroy it.

Vitamin B_2 is necessary to keep the skin and oral mucosa of mouth healthy. It also plays part in the normal functioning of the eyes and promoting carbohydrate metabolism. Yeast, liver, milk, cheese, curd, pulses, peas, beans, green leafy vegetables, egg, meat, and whole grain cereals are its richest sources.

Vitamin B_6 inhibits the production of cholesterol and helps in break-down of fats, proteins and carbohydrates, and is necessary for maintaining healthy skin, a good digestive tract and sound mental health. It is obtained from fish, meat, fowl, potato, whole grain, yeast, tomato, groundnut and green vegetables.

Vitamin B_9 ensures good growth of the body, and formation and maturation of red blood cells. Green leafy vegetables, yeast, banana, sprouted pulses, cauliflower, meat, liver and kidney are rich in its supply. Over-cooking destroys it.

Vitamin B_{12} is essential for the formation of healthy erythrocytes, and myelin, as well as for proper growth of the body. Its major sources are meat, liver, fish, egg, milk and cheese.

Vitamin C helps in collagen-formation. It is essential for keeping teeth, gums, and body joints healthy. It increases body-resistance to infection and holds body cells together. It is richly found in citrus fruit like lemon, orange, lime, etc., *amla*, gooseberry, guava, tomatoes, peppers, leafy green vegetables especially cabbage, potatoes. Vitamin C gets destroyed by heat and light. It gets oxidized when cut-fruits are left exposed to air for a long time.

Vitamin D is necessary for normal growth of bones and teeth. We get it profusely from milk, egg yolk, fish-liver oil, butter, margarine, liver, and fish. Vitamin D is also manufactured in the body when the skin is exposed to sunlight. It facilitates absorption of calcium and phosphorus by intestine and their retention in the body and their utilization for bone and teeth formation.

Vitamin E acts as anti-oxidant and protects lipids of cell membranes against oxygen damage. Thus it prevents breakage of RBCs. It ensures normal reproduction, normal functioning of muscles and protection of the liver. Green leafy vegetables, milk, butter, whole cereal grains, vegetable oils, liver and tomatoes are its major sources. Heat destroys it.

Vitamin K is necessary for normal clotting of blood and preventing hemorrhage. It is also essential for the normal functioning of the liver. It is derived from green leafy vegetables such as radish top, coriander, cabbage, spinach, etc., tomatoes, soybean oil and liver. It is also synthesized in the body by the intestinal bacteria. The prolonged use of sulfa drugs and antibiotics destroys it.

Minerals

Besides the food constituents listed above, body also requires certain inorganic substances such as metals, non-metals and their salts; all put together known as *minerals*, which form 4 percent of the body weight. In all, there are 21 minerals, considered very essential for normal health. Each mineral plays a direct specific role in the structure and function of the body. No mineral can be a substitute for any other mineral; its deficiency adversely affects the growth and reproduction.

Minerals may function in the body in several ways:

- as constituents of bone, teeth, giving rigidity to the skeleton;
- as essential elements of protoplasm associated with enzyme activity;
- as soluble constituents of the fluids of the body influencing the elasticity and irritability of the muscles and nerves, supplying material for the acidity or alkalinity of the body fluids, helping to maintain the acid-base equilibrium of the body fluids as well as their osmotic characteristics and solvent power; and probably in many other ways.

Minerals supply no energy to the body but without them several functions of the body cannot occur. Not only must the body be supplied with required minerals, essential for its functions, but also they must be supplied in readily absorbable form. Our body can use them in the compound form and not as pure elements. For instance, we cannot eat sodium metal or chlorine gas in their elemental form because they are poisonous but their compound sodium chloride is a mineral salt - harmless and essential for the body.

There are seven major minerals viz. calcium, phosphorus, potassium, sulphur, sodium, chlorine and magnesium, and nine minor ones such as iodine, iron, zinc, manganese, copper, cobalt, fluorine, molybdenum and selenium. The rest five are needed in very small quantity. Minerals are supplied to the body by the food we eat.

Calcium is a constituent of all protoplasm and of body fluids. 99% of it is in our bones and teeth. It plays significant role in blood clotting, muscle contraction, heart function and action of several enzymes and hormones. Milk, milk products such as cheese, hard water, green leafy vegetables, carrots, beans, whole gram, cereals, meat, fish, tapioca, etc., are its chief sources. Growing children and lactating mothers require large amounts of calcium. Human body cannot adapt to calcium shortage.

Phosphorus is essential for the normal development of bones and teeth. It helps in maintaining the constant composition of the body fluids and enzymes and their functioning. Its chief sources are milk, cheese, green leafy vegetables, oatmeal, nuts, liver, kidney, bajra, ragi, etc.

Potassium content of the body is about 125 gm, and is found primarily inside the cells where it functions in association with various enzymes. It is intimately connected with the contraction of the skeletal and cardiac muscles, transmission of nerve impulse, and maintenance of the electrolyte balance in the body. Its sources are widely distributed in all foods. Excess or subnormal amount of potassium causes immediate mal-functioning of the heart.

Sodium and *Chlorine* are necessary to maintain the osmotic pressure of the body fluids. Obtained largely from common salts, fish, meat, eggs and milk, they are associated with the muscle contraction, transmission of nerve impulse and maintenance of positive electrolyte balance in the body.

Iodine is utilized by the thyroid gland in the synthesis of thyroxin, the deficiency of which causes goitre. Its major sources are drinking water, onion, marine fish, seafood and iodized table salt.

The body needs ***Iron*** to manufacture haemoglobin, which is present in red blood cells, and also for oxidation of tissues. Liver, kidney, eggs, molasses, oatmeal, apricot, guava, raisins, groundnuts, spinach, green leafy vegetables, bajra, ragi, etc., are very rich in iron content. The deficiency of iron in the body causes anaemia.

A diet furnishing sufficient carbohydrates, fats and proteins may sometimes be lacking in calcium, iron, phosphorus, iodine, and copper unless vegetables and fruits are added adequately to prevent this deficiency.

Roughage

Not all food we eat gets digested; some of it is left undigested, which may primarily be a waste but it does serve some important purpose in the entire process of digestion and absorption. Indigestible fibrous material in the food is known as roughage, such as ***cellulose*** in fruits and vegetables and ***connective tissue*** in meat and fish. These things contain no energy; they nevertheless help the digestive system to perform its functions efficiently. By consuming vegetables, fruits and other plant material, we take in a large quantity of cellulose. Unfortunately the human body does not have enzymes to digest the cellulose carbohydrates. Due to this reason, cellulose of our body remains undigested. This, being a fibrous material, acts as roughage and keeps the digestive system in perfect order.

Roughage bears a lot of water and helps in retaining it in the body. Being bulky, it expands the intestines as it moves through them so that the passage of food becomes smoother. People having adequate roughage in their food, suffer no pangs of constipation.

Salad vegetables and fruits with skin and high fibre content provide enough roughage. Corncob, unpeeled apple and half-crushed wheat are also rich in roughage content.

Water

Water is rightly called the "elixir of life" because a person dies sooner if he is deprived of it. Surprisingly, water is no food but an inorganic compound of the atoms of hydrogen and oxygen. It supplies no energy to the body as carbohydrates or fats do, nor does it help building body tissue as proteins do; it only helps preparing food for assimilation by the body. About 65 to 75 percent of human body is all water.

Water performs the following functions in the human body:

(1) It regulates the body temperature through sweating and evaporation. When the outside temperature rises, water oozes out through our skin in the form of sweat.

(2) It provides channel for excretion of waste products of the body. As it evaporates from the skin, it takes away latent heat so that the skin cools down and we feel good.

(3) The essential biochemical reactions are carried out in the body through the medium of water only.

(4) As it is a good solvent, all the salts and dissolved nutrients are transported to their intended sites in the body through water alone.

(5) Water is an excellent lubricant. It is present in the fluids where organs and bones rub against one another during movement so as to lessen the impact of friction and avoid injury.

The human requirement for water depends on age, type of activity, season and climatic conditions. Almost all vegetables and fruit we eat supply some quantity of water but most of the water we consume comes from plain "drinking water", tea, coffee, milk, fruit juice, cold drinks, etc. A small amount of water is also produced by the oxidation of glucose during respiration. A state of *dehydration* prevails when an abnormal depletion of body fluids or excessive loss water from the tissues of the body occurs.

Man's Dietary Requirements

Diet is the kind of food on which an individual or a group of individual lives. A ***balanced diet,*** to recapitulate, is defined as one which contains a variety of foods in such quantities and proportions that the need for energy, amino acids, vitamins, minerals, fats, carbohydrate and other nutrients is adequately met for maintaining health, vitality and general wellbeing and also make a small provision for extra nutrients to withstand short duration of leanness. A balanced diet has become an accepted means to safeguard a population from malnutrition, ill-health, disability and disease. Normally human body requires carbohydrates, proteins and fats in the proportion of 4 : 1 : 1 with adequate amount of minerals (salts), vitamins and roughage. A balanced diet provides food materials for all the metabolic requirements of the body energy, growth, repair and replacement of the worn-out tissues and physiological regulation. Remember, all essential constituents of a balanced diet are obtained from cereals, pulses, oils, milk, meat, vegetables, fruits, etc.

A wholesome meal is a basic requirement for all. However, dietary requirements of an individual are influenced by his age, sex, state of health and occupation. A growing child requires more of proteins than an adult who needs more of fats and carbohydrates for energy to do hard physical work. Vitamins and minerals are also needed in greater quantity for children than older people. Normally girls require less food than boys and a pregnant woman requires a special care in respect of her dietary requirement. She needs more proteins in her daily diet in order to nourish the growing embryo inside her. The requirement of carbohydrates, minerals and vitamins also goes up considerably during pregnancy for obvious reasons. Lactating or nursing mothers need special diet, which ought to be rich in proteins, calcium and vitamins. This will meet their own requirements and those of the growing child. Occupation or the type of work one does is a very important factor in determining man's dietary requirements. The diet of farm hand, wood chopper, an athlete, or a cart-puller has to be significantly rich in carbohydrates and fats than a businessman, a university professor or a scientist whose lifestyle, more or less, is sedentary. Consuming too rich a food without correspondingly engaging in energy-consuming work adds to one's weight, leads to obesity, and makes a person vulnerable to cardiovascular complications. Besides, there is a difference in the diet of a healthy individual and that of a patient or the person recuperating after a prolonged sickness. Such an individual would require easily digestible soups, fruits, vegetables, oil and fat free diet such as bread, rice, etc.,

The ***Indian Council of Medical Research*** has recommended the following diet for adult men and women (each item in gm.)

	Adult Men			Adult Women		
Food Item	*Sedentary*	*Moderate work*	*Heavy work*	*Sedentary*	*Moderate work*	*Heavy*
Cereals	460	520	670	410	440	575
Pulses	40	50	60	40	45	50
Leafy Veg.	40	40	40	100	100	50
Other Veg.	60	70	80	40	40	100
Roots & Tubers	50	60	80	50	50	60
Milk	150	200	250	100	150	200
Oil & Fat	40	45	65	20	25	40
Sugar or Jaggery	30	35	55	20	20	40
Fruits	30	40	65	30	40	60

MALNUTRITION AND ADULTERATION

Along with insanitation, passive or sedentary life-style, high speed traffic, and noise, air and water pollution, the two greatest man-made hazards that threaten human health and life with incalculable risk are malnutrition and adulteration.

While malnutrition – the lack of proper nutrition required for maintaining good health – may generally be due to natural or economic causes, adulteration is squarely due to man's selfishness and greed to make money by dishonest means by mixing the food stuffs with something inferior or spurious.

All over the Globe, millions of people, particularly in the Third Word countries, live in abject poverty, filth and squalor and suffer from a variety of deadly diseases (especially deficiency diseases) due to malnutrition. Even in some developed and developing countries hundreds of thousands of people are the victim of malnutrition due mainly to two major reasons: economic backwardness and lack of proper education about health and nutrition. Situation is not at all bright in our country as well. In the most literate State like Kerala, almost 40% of people especially women, irrespective of their caste, creed or region, are victim of anaemia (bloodlessness: lack of red blood corpuscles or of haemoglobin) – a condition marked by paleness and languor, which affects their capacity to stay at work and is the major cause of poor productivity. In some cases it may lead to other health complications.

Like malnutrition, adulteration is also wide spread in several countries especially where there is rampant exploitation of the common man by the business community and State administration remains a silent spectator to wide spread ill-health and death due to the consumption of adulterated food stuff or other material used by people. In countries like Singapore and United States there are very strict laws governing purity of food and no one can dare play with the health and life of the people by adulterating food material.

Concept of Malnutrition and its implication in Human Health

Malnutrition (meaning faulty or imperfect nutrition) refers to a state of failure to achieve a minimal intake of nutrients for maintaining health the cause of which generally lies in quantitative or qualitative deficiencies. Depending of the degree and amount of deficiency of a food constituent, the ability of the individual to digest, absorb, or otherwise process ingested food may be badly affected resulting in ill-health or even death in the long run.

Causes of Malnutrition

The causes of malnutrition are well documented but they may differ from place to place and from country to country. In general, the major causes, however, are listed below:

1. *Defective heredity* due to which some people find it difficult to digest certain food material such as milk, which is a near perfect food, resulting in severe health complications in life. This is true about majority of people in many parts of Africa, and many Asians as well.
2. *Economic backwardness* (especially abject poverty, inability to invest in nutrition) leaves little scope for millions of people to manage even square meals, not to talk of nutritious food.
3. *Lack of proper education* about principles and composition of a balanced diet; most people, including very well-educated ones, know little about what to eat. They wake up only after great damage to their health has already occurred.
4. *Bad eating habits* especially with the urban people who have developed great taste for fast (virtually junk) food. Obesity is much rampant in urban people than those living in rural areas.
5. *Sedentary life style* is another cause of malnutrition; since people do not engage in adequate physical work even in routines, so they are not in a position to have appetite for rich balanced diet.
6. *Non-availability of nutritious food material* in a particular area. This is a natural scarcity and is difficult to make up. People have to continue to live with it until they can find a substitute for it. In

normal conditions, we do not get all nutritious stuff in our vicinity and it is impossible to import it in large quantity.

7. *Wrongly developed tastes* are also responsible for nutrition deficiency; we have developed tastes for certain dishes even if their nutritious value is almost zero. This is very true about young children who develop tastes for certain types of food stuffs (bakery items, chips, French fries, fried items, etc.) and sacrifice eating green leafy vegetables, salads, fruits etc., that meet our nutrition requirements so well.
8. *Outdated customs and traditions*, quite often, strike at the root of our nutrition. Sticking to family or community traditions, we get used to cooking and eating our food in certain traditionally typical styles (over-cooking, deep-frying, roasting to the point of burning) and by unscientific processes so that the food stuff loses nutritional value.
9. *Climatic and geographical conditions* may also be responsible for nutritional deficiency in their diet. For example, the subsoil water in an area may not be fit for human consumption; it may be too alkaline, soft or hard or may have excess quantity of calcium or potassium. All this is responsible for a state of imperfection in human diet.
10. *Inability of the under-developed countries to increase their agricultural resources* or *develop an industrial economy* may, well be related to the food shortages that result in malnutrition of their people, leaving them weak and low fit for productive work.

Health Implications of Malnutrition

As a rule, *we are literally what we eat.* This does not mean that the substance of our body is made up of the basic unit building blocks that come in with our ingested food or that we are dependent on what we eat for energy to drive our *living engine* – our body. Far more, it means that our ability to function well, our personality, outlook and sense of well-being, and even our capacity to learn and develop are related to the food we eat.

Effect of Vitamin Deficiency

It is now a common knowledge that most deficiency diseases are caused by lack of vitamins and mineral salts in human diet. The benefits of taking vitamins to build up body resistance to disease and avoid serious deficiencies have been explained. However, it would be apt to throw some light on deleterious effects of lack of various vitamins in food as observed in malnutrition and defective growth, as shown below:

Name	Function	Result of Deficiency
Lipid-Soluble Vitamins		
Vitamin A	Called growth vitamin, it maintain integrity of epithelial tissues; needed as part of visual purple in retina of eye.	Xerophthalmia (dry cornea, no tear secretion, phryrnodermia (toad skin), night blindness, growth retardation.
Vitamin D	Regulates metabolism of calcium and phosphorus; promotes absorption of calcium in intestine; needed for normal growth and mineralization of bones.	Rickets in young (bones soft, yielding, often deformed); ostomalacia (soft bones), especially in women in Asia.
Vitamin E	Anti-oxidative; maintains integrity of membranes.	Degeneration of testes with failure to produce sperms; embryonic growth disturbances, suckling paralysis and muscular dystrophy in young animals.
Vitamin K	Essential to production of prothombin in liver, necessary for blood clotting.	Blood fails to clot resulting in hemorrhages.
Water-soluble Vitamins		
Vitamin B complex (B_1) Thiamine	Needed for carbohydrate metabolism.	Variety of symptoms of health disturbance such as loss appetite, with loss of tone and reduced mobility in digestive tract; cessation of growth; beri beri (nerve inflammation).

(B_2) Riboflavin	Essential for growth; forms prosthetic group of FAD enzymes concerned with immediate metabolism of food and electron-transport system.	Inflammation of lips, scales on ears, cracks in the lips, and at the corners of the mouth, swelling of the tongue, and certain disturbances of the eyes.
Niacin (also called Nicotinic acid)	Forms active group of nicotinamide adenine denucleotide, which functions in dehydrogenation reactions.	Pellegra (weakness, lack of appetite, indigestion and a skin rash at the beginning followed by ulcerations of the mouth and diarrhea.
Foli cacid	Essential for growth of and formation of blood cells; coenzyme involved in transfer of single-carbon units in metabolism.	Anaemia, hemorrhage from kidneys, and spruce (defective intestinal absorption).
(B_6) Pyridoxine	Essential for normal growth and nutrition, and in its active form is important for functioning of several enzyme systems.	Dermatitis; growth retardation.
Pantothenic acid	Essential for the intermediate metabolism of fats, carbohydrates and certain amino acids; forms coenzymes A. which is involved in the formation of cholesterol and the steroid hormones, also of acetycholine, which is essential for transmission of nerve impulses.	Deficiencies rarely occur in man but dermatitis with thickening of skin in rats and chicks.
Biotin (Vitamin H)	Essential for growth; functions in CO2 fixation and fatty acid oxidation and synthesis.	Dermatitis with thickening of skin in rats and chick; perosis in birds.
(B_{12}) Cynaocobalamin	Formation of blood cells, growth; coenzyme involved in transfer of methyl groups and in nucleic acid metabolism.	Pernicious anaemia, slow growth in young animals; wasting disease in ruminants.

Vitamin C or ascorbic acid	Maintains integrity of capillary walls; involved in formation of "inter-cellular cement"; formation blood cells in the bone marrow.	Scurvy (bleeding in muscous membranes, under skin, and into joints) in humans and guinea pigs; impaired general nutrition;prevent healing of wounds; lower general resistance of the body.

Effect of Deficiency of Essential Compounds

Though most dramatic of the deficiency diseases are those associated with specific vitamin deficiencies, malnutrition is not limited to this alone. Insufficient amount of essential compounds in diet may also cause deficiency diseases. Carbon, hydrogen and oxygen are always found in fats, carbohydrates and proteins in abundance but availability of nitrogen is found only in protein, and this explains why health cannot be maintained on a diet of only carbohydrates and fats. General starvation in which caloric needs are not met by sufficient intake of carbohydrates and fats is life-threatening but not wide spread, except in some parts of the developing world. In Africa, *marasmas* is a disease characterized by slow starvation. In many cases sufficient calories are taken in to prevent death through starvation, but specific nutrients are lacking or dangerously low in amount. Fairly common in sub-Sahara Africa, *kwashiorkor* is a deficiency disease in which protein is inadequate. Unfortunately foods rich in protein such as beef and pork are much more expensive than those high in carbohydrate and even fat. Even if caloric needs are being met, long-term deprivation of protein will result in the breakdown of tissue and lost of vital structures,

Effect of Deficiency of Mineral Salts

Most mineral salts - sodium chloride, phosphorus, magnesium, iron, etc. - are contained in sufficient amounts in food without any care in selection for this purpose. Amount of sodium chloride added in food is more than sufficient for the body needs; potassium and magnesium are fairly abundant in meat (muscles) and in vegetables so that an ordinary mixed diet with some roughage will contain sufficient amounts of these substances. Important information with regard to major mineral salts is given below:

- *Calcium* is essential for cellular activities. It is related to normal permeability of cellular membranes, excitability of muscle, normal heart action and never activity, and must be present in ionic form for normal blood clotting. It is a constituent of all protoplasm and of body fluids and is present in large proportions in bones and teeth. These body processes may be badly affected in the absence of calcium in required quantity.
- *Phosphorus* is essential to the normal development of bones and teeth. It is a necessary constituent of all cells, particularly nerve and muscle cells. Its inadequate supply retard growth and maintenance of bones and teeth.
- *Magnesium* is a vital element in cell physiology because it serves as a co-factor in the metabolism of glucose, pyruvic acid, and of adenosine triphosphate. In excessive amounts it has a depressing action on nerve transmission and nerve tissue functioning in general.
- *Potassium* is intimately concerned with transmission of the nerve impulse, with skeletal muscle contraction, and with cardiac contraction. Its excess quantity causes mal-functioning of the heart.
- The presence of *Iron* in the haemoglobin enables the latter to attract oxygen and carry it to the cells. Iron deficiency, which is especially more in women, affects work efficiency and staying power at job.
- *Iodine* is utilized by the thyroid gland in the synthesis of thyroxin, the adequate supply of which is necessary for keeping the occurrence of goitre at bay.

Adulteration and its Effect on Health

Meaning of Adulteration

Adulteration is an act of *mixing the food stuff with something inferior or spurious,* in order to make illegitimate profit. The intentional addition or substitution or abstraction of substances which adversely affect the nature, substance and quality of food stuff, is an unpardonable crime against humanity. This world-wide phenomenon - more particularly rampant in the under-developed countries - makes innocent people victim of human greed, and jeopardizes their health, some time leading to untimely deaths.

Food Adulteration Tricks

Some of the common tricks used by the business tycoons to adulterate food items of daily consumption are enumerated below:

1. Mixing rice with white (marble) stone chips to increase bulk of the commodity. It is no surprise at all.
2. Adding water to milk and selling it as cow's or goat's milk is a common practice these days. More hazardous to human health than this is to mix drain water or chalk water, or starches with milk.
3. Mixing mashed potato, sweet potato and other starched material in butter or *khoya.*
4. Adding cheap edible oil(s) to vanaspati ghee or mixing perfumed vanaspati ghee with pure (*desi*) ghee and selling it at sky-rocketing price.
5. Using artificial dyes for colouring tea leaves so that the stuff looks genuine.
6. Adding extraneously coloured cheap or useless substances to turmeric and chilly powder.
7. Mixing powdered rice bran, wheat husk and/or saw dust with spices.
8. Horse dung dry powder mixing with the coriander powder, is a usual practice.

9. Mixing grass seeds coloured with charcoal dust in cumin seeds (black zeera).
10. Mixing resin, gum, colour, soap stones or some unspecified earth material with Asapoeida (Heeng).
11. Preparing spurious liquor from out of spirit or some other drugs and mixing it either with genuine one or selling it as genuine. Every day scores of cases of death or ill-health due to consumption of illicit liquor, are reported in the media. In most cases the victims are the underdogs (people living below poverty line).
12. Life-saving drugs and medicines are sometimes found adulterated in several cases even though the laws to this effect are seemingly so strict.

National Safeguards against Food Adulteration

It may just not be possible to make a complete list of the food items that generally strike the market in an adulterated form because every day new techniques of adulterating food stuff are being invented and new materials being discovered for this purpose. Adulteration has become a cancerous activity in our country even though standards of food stuff are governed by the following Act/Order of the Government of India:

1. Prevention of Food Adulteration Act, 1954.
2. Fruit Products (Amendment) Order, 1961.

Apart from the statutory food standards prescribed in the Act/Order quoted above, standards for ensuring the quality of different categories of food products are not mandatory, which leaves more than enough scope for the *thugs* and exploiters to manipulate the provisions in the Act/Order to their advantage and make fortune without being apprehended and punished for the risk they pose to the common populace. Though the Prevention of Food Adulteration Act and its Amendment are intended to make it incumbent on the manufacturers and traders to ensure good quality of products they market, numerous visible or invisible lacunae in the provisions of the Act/Order make the whole show an exercise in futility.

Effect of Adulteration on Health

Adulteration of food affects health of the people in several ways:

1. Some people lose their lives by consuming adulterated food, especially non-vegetarian dishes and hard drinks, because a variety of spurious additions to food stuff may contain poisonous substances.
2. People may slowly contract certain known and unknown diseases as they would hardly know as to what kind of stuff they are eating.
3. They may suffer from numerous health problems such as allergies, tuberculosis, diarrhea, gastro-enteritis, indigestion, and so on, because it is only after consumption they would know whether there was something wrong with the food they had ingested.
4. Children are the worst sufferer of food adulteration because not only will their life energies lose vitality but also they may have retarded physical and mental growth and development.
5. Consumption of spurious medicines may do little to cure a patient despite best prescription and also put the physician to dilemma; the adulterated stuff may not enable a patient to recover from the illness speedily.
6. Economic loss on account of adulterated food the consumption is likely to create psychological problems for the victims of adulteration. No wonder such people suffer from acute mental disorders.
7. When a large number of people suffer from food adulteration, the nation virtually gets a bad name and its reputation is badly bruised. Its hopes to produce healthy, fit and strong defenders of its borders and boundaries are dashed to the ground.

A Wise Advice

A wise advice given to the people by the Government (especially the Consumers' Forum) with breathless repetition through print and electronic media is to buy food stuff and goods that bear *Agmark, ISI, or FPO* labels. This will go a long way in fighting the food adulteration menace to some extent otherwise it is impossible to wipe out this malady from the society.

QUESTIONS FOR EXERCISE

Short-answer Questions

On the basis of the model for answering short-answer questions at the end of Chapter-1, answer the following questions as precisely as possible.

1. Explain the importance of health in life.
2. On what does quality of life depend?
3. Why health is a wide concept?
4. Write five sentences on health as the most valuable possession of man.
5. What is the concept of health in *Ayurveda* – the Hindu science of health?
6. What does health, in general, mean?
7. From the WHO viewpoint, what does health mean?
8. Give a simple but precise definition of health.
9. List the major dimensions of health.
10. What does mental or emotion dimension of health stand for?
11. Explain briefly the social dimension of health.
12. Why prevention of disease is more important than its cure?
13. What does environment do to our health?
14. Define health education in your own words.
15. Give the major aim of health education at school.
16. How does a loving mother educate her child in its health habits?
17. Where does health education derive its substance from?
18. How is health education a universal education?
19. Why is it not possible to define health education in absolute terms?
20. Give a precise definition of health education?
21. Precisely enumerate the salient characteristics of health education.
22. List the major objectives of health education.
23. Define health instruction in your own words.
24. What is health supervision and how does it help in improving health of the children?
25. Give short write-up on health environment.
26. Why health education is a strong motivation?
27. Write three major principles of health education.

28. How is health education a cooperative affair?
29. Why competent leadership is necessary for health education?
30. Why is health education a science of practical utility?
31. Define a balanced diet.
32. Enumerate various elements of a balanced diet.
33. What function does food perform in our body?
34. What are three major considerations in the matter of nutrition?
35. How has our notion of normal nutrition changed over the years?
36. What are the characteristics of under-nourished people?
37. Give the proportions of carbohydrates, fat and protein in a good diet?
38. Give the composition of a wholesome daily diet.
39. Name the energy-yielding foods.
40. Explain the function of carbohydrates in the body.
41. What is importance of fats as the richest source of energy?
42. What happens when we take more calories than we can burn them?
43. From what foods do we get maximum carbohydrates?
44. What functions do proteins perform in our body?
45. List out sources of plant proteins and animal proteins.
46. What are vitamins and do they do to our body?
47. Give the sources and benefits of vitamin A.
48. Where from do we obtain vitamin B complex?
49. Give the importance of vitamin C and D for human body.
50. What functions do minerals perform in our body?
51. What would happen to our body if iron were not present in out diet?
52. Throw light on the importance of roughage in our body.
53. Give the dietary requirements of a common man.
54. Explain malnutrition in your own words.
55. Give a proper definition of adulteration.
56. How does malnutrition affect human growth and development?
57. Enumerate five causes of malnutrition.
58. Why malnutrition and adulteration are considered as the great enemies of man's health?
59. What is the effect of the deficiency of mineral salts on human body?
60. What are national safeguards against food adulteration?

CHAPTER: THREE

BIOLOGICAL BASIS OF PHYSICAL EDUCATION

As an academic and research subject, physical education is defined as *science of movement*. Human movement is no ordinary mechanical movement but a movement performed by an unparalleled self-powered, self-driven, self-motivated and self-sustaining complex *thinking* machine. In order to understand and analyze human movement with a view to improve man's functional efficiency and performance in various areas of interaction including sports, we may have to peep into a number of biological sciences.

The foundational assumptions of the theory of physical education are rooted in several biological sciences like zoology, biology, anthropometry, anatomy, physiology, anthropology, kinesiology, behaviour sciences, etc., - to mention a few. As an overview of the view-points put up by these sciences, there is adequate evidence to emphasize that human movement cannot be understood without reference to important discoveries by biologists, anthropologists, psychologists and others concerning evolution of animal species in general and *homo sapiens* in particular.

Biological Facts about Man and his Movement

Man and his movement are the product of biological evolution. There is a long history of evolution and the transformations his body and movement under went in order to come to the present state. A few important facts derived from biology have serious implication in physical education:

- The origin of life on the Earth and the evolution of species was more a matter of systematic but unbelievably long evolution rather than an act of Providence, as expostulated in several religious scriptures of the world.

- Like other organisms, man also evolved from a single-celled organism and acquired the status of an extremely complex being after passing through numerous evolutionary stages in his structure and function.
- The evolutionary process that has been very slow and spanned over billions of years has brought about gradual, though sometimes sudden and catastrophic, changes in the structure and function of animals, thereby transforming the creation and giving rise to an endless variety of animal species with peculiar characteristics - man being no exception to it.
- According to biologists, the major factors which assisted the transition from ape to man were *natural selection, mitosis* (the process of cell reproduction of cells through cell division), *meiosis* of the sex cell or sexual selection, *use and disuse* of organs, *environmental changes,* and other correlative changes.
- As a result of several correlative factors and conditions, the *hominoid* (ape-like man) left arboreal (living on trees) life, assumed upright posture (becoming biped in place of quadruped) and developed new parts of the brain (cerebrum), thereby assuming the shape and size of a distinct and intelligent *human* species.
- Charles Darwin – the author of Evolution of Species and Struggle for Existence hypotheses – firmly believed: "In the course of evolution, man's ancestors lost certain characteristics either fully or in part; a keen sense of smell, the hairy covering on the body, the majority of the dermal muscles, the tail, the prehensile (fast moving) feet, pointed ear

lobes, etc." In discussing the causes that led man to adopt erect mode of locomotion, Darwin felt that *change of feeding* was of greatest importance.

- The *upright posture* brought about such consequential changes in man as greater range of mobility in the joints, movement variability especially of the upper limbs, structural and functional adjustments, evolution of an intelligent brain superimposing over the reptilian and mammalian brain structures, enabling man to usher in Cultural Revolution.
- Though no perceptible changes seem to have occurred to man and his movement during the last 30, 000 years or so, it is incorrect to presume that biological evolution has hit the dead-end of the road; it is still going on.
- It is important to note that first man made the greatest use of his *muscle* for survival and search for food but with the development of intelligent brain, he leaned greatly on his intelligence and began to use his *brain* more than his brawn in interacting with the environment and dealing with changing life situations.
- Importantly, human body structure and its function, his movement, his growth and development, activities, behaviours, etc., have been significantly conditioned by the biological forces over hundreds of millennia; they are ultimately controlled, directed and governed by the laws of nature.

All these and many more facts of biology occupy an important place in the theory of science of movement especially where the aim of physical education has in its central focus the organic development (motor control, fitness and functional efficiency of the body organs and systems), development of neuromuscular skills and development of a harmonious personality (synchronized growth of the body and development of the mind).

MEANING OF GROWTH & DEVELOPMENT

Almost all living organisms are structurally complete at birth. They acquire no additional organs in during their life span. However, functionally they become more complex as they interact with the environment. The structural transformation and differentiation which consequently follow cannot be simply termed growth. The qualitative change in structure due to function and vice-versa is called development. ***Growth and development, therefore, comprise a series of orderly and irreversible stages that each and every organism goes through from the onset of life to the end.***

It is common for people to use the terms growth and development interchangeably. Without going into etymological genesis of the words, suffice to say that growth is one aspect of development and refers to the increase caused by biological process in which the organism becomes bigger in size, volume and heavier in weight. Starting his life almost from an invisible dot, the human organism grows to be more than five feet in height and more than 150 pounds in weight. Growth indicates enlargement of cells, fibres and muscles, elongation of the skeleton and increase in the general volume of the body. Growth brings about perceptible changes in structure and form. It is quantitative in the sense that it can be measured in inches and points. Marked by structural changes, an adolescent is easily distinguishable from an infant and an adult from an adolescent. The growth curve moves upward up to a certain age, levels off and stabilizes.

In comparison to growth, development is a much wider term indicating advancement, more unfoldment, a progressive change, a sort of growing forward to greater maturity. Being a process of qualitative transformation, development is more than a concept. It can be observed, appraised and even measured in three major manifestations: (a) anatomic, (b) physiologic, and (c) behavioural....... Behaviour signs, however, constitute a most comprehensive index of developmental states and developmental potential. Development specifically refers to characteristic change in the efficiency of the organs and organ-systems. For instance, the bones not only elongate with passage of time but also ossify, harden, get stronger and are able to bear more weight. Similarly, heart increases in size; it also becomes more efficient in its out-put (pumping more blood) and stroke volume. According to Benedict, development is a "process in which the internal physiological change and the psychological processes stimulated by them are integrated (or responded to) in a way which enables the individual to master further and anew, environmental stimulations."

Growth and development are like two sides of a coin. Physical development does not necessarily mean increase in size. There are modifications of the body-composition taking place constantly. In the body, for example, gain in weight comes partly from increase in neural, glandular, and muscle tissue; in childhood the gain comes principally from bone and muscle tissue, while in adult years, the gain is from and accumulation of fat tissue. Normally growth comes to its dead-end by the time a boy or girl crosses "teens", development continues further depending upon quality of nutrition, life-style, type of work one perform as a vocation, environmental pressures (stresses), etc. While growth is largely physical, development encompasses intellectual and social qualities including knowledge, skills and experiences. Growth is solid, observable and measurable, development is an abstract concept; it is observed and measured indirectly. Growth is marked by objectivity, development by subjectivity-objectivity. The height of a child is periodically measured in centimetres, the functional ability of the muscles is recorded through measurement of shape and strength - qualitative and quantitative measures. Scientists have devised numerous tests of motor-ability, physical fitness, intellectual abilities, psychomotor qualities, etc., with a view to objectify the developmental changes taking place in an individual from time to time. Yet sociability, cooperation, team spirit, character etc., are left to be judged subjectively by parents, teachers, elders, seniors and superiors. Development, therefore, manifests a much broader perspective than growth.

Despite this, neither growth nor development can be discussed without reference to each other because both processes are so closely knit that they cannot be formally disentangled and separated.

FACTORS AFFECTING GROWTH & DEVELOPMENT

Growth is a creative process in as much as it adds something to the physical, mental, intellectual and behavioural dimensions of a child minute by minute, day by day, month by month and year by year. In fact, growth brings irreversible transformation in the child. Marked changes are seen in the structure, function and behaviour of the child as its growth curve moves up with advancement in years. An infant is significantly different from a new-born baby, a child from an infant, an adolescent from a child, and so on. Apart from this, there are individual differences in growth among individuals - even among siblings and twins - despite the fact that the general pattern of growth and development of children irrespective of race, religion, language or geographical location, by and large, remains the same. This law of nature is unalterable.

Growth and development are very dynamic processes. They are influenced by hundreds of visible and invisible factors and forces - some natural, some genetic, some individual, some social and some cultural. Fluctuation in a child's growth is an irrefutable fact because there are periods of slow growth and periods of accelerated growth in case of each and every child; generally, the early childhood and puberty are periods of fast growth, and later childhood and later adolescence periods of consolidation (slow growth). This arrangement is natural and is impossible to alter. However, growth is significantly influenced both negatively and positively by hundreds of external and internal factors, conditions and forces. While good nutrition, generally congenial environment, good habits, physical exercise and overall content and happiness are quite conducive to growth, prominent hazards of growth include malnutrition, disease, endocrinal dys-functioning, environmental pollution, psychosomatic disorders, inactive life-style, lack of physical exercise, etc.

The factors influencing growth and development can be categorized into (a) hereditary or genetic factors, and (b) environmental factors.

Growth Influencing Factors - Heredity

Heredity is an invisible complex force and it determines that the new individual is to be *human*, but it also determines the particular kind of human that will result at birth. The basic physical and mental make-up of an individual as well as the pattern of his growth and development are closely related to heredity and governed by the laws of inheritance - the invisible force of nature. The heredity that parents give is passed on to the offspring (children) through the genes present in the chromosomes. The genetic structure is transmitted from one generation to another by the DNA (deoxyribonucleic acids) of which the genes are made. The outward evidences of inheritance such as eye colour, shape of nose, stature and general bodily conformation, as well as inward traits, such as intelligence, resistance to disease and quality of tissue are expressions of gene activity.

If the parental genes are defective in any trait, the child is likely to have the particular trait defective. Physical structure, stature, eye-colour and quality of hair, as well as traits of behaviour such as laziness, quick temper, cruelty, self-reliance and methodical carefulness are subject to this law. It needs to be noted that the genes carry only what they possess. Variations do occur in the transmission of heredity traits depending upon which of the two immediate parents carries the defective gene and in what trait. However, diseases, disorders and defects transmitted genetically may not be cured or corrected with the help of external forces; they become permanent property of an individual's personality. There is no dearth of instances where children brought up under most uncongenial environmental conditions such as malnutrition, work stress, etc., reached the usual physical stature of the family later. Height-weight patterns, complexion, susceptibility to certain diseases (such as colour blindness, haemophilia - a constitutional tendency to excessive bleeding when any blood-vessel is even slightly injured - feeble-mindedness, submissiveness, etc.) psychosomatic disorders, physiological capacities, etc., are significantly influenced by hereditary factors and genetic make-up.

The influence of heredity on human growth and development can be seen in the predisposition of the American and most European children to grow taller and heavier as compared to their Asian counterparts. Due to heredity only, an average European person is more heavily built than an Indian or a Chinese; the Negroes have wavy thick hair, big nose and black complexion, and the Mongolian race people have slit eyes and a small flat nose. It is impossible to alter the pattern of the growth an individual has inherited from his parents, grandparents and great grandparents, and so on. Those who guarantee increase in the height of a person with external mechanism (medicine or exercise) are the greatest tricksters. Now-a-days hormonal therapy is taking giant strides in attempts to find out permanent cure for some inherited defects.

Growth Influencing Factors - Environment

If heredity is complex, so is environment. Environment encompasses two aspects: the physical and the social. The physical environment constitutes the world of nature (surroundings, mountains, lakes, shelters, fauna and flora, roads, buildings, industry, factories, business complexes, etc.), and the social environment refers to people - family, parents, neighbours, school mates, friends, and other significant people - and their ideas, customs, traditions, etc. While heredity is an internal force, environmental is external and contains everything that hereditary does not and comes from outside the human body.

There are hundreds of big and small factors, forces and conditions that in one way or the other affect, mould, and alter the growth and development patterns of an individual. Here it would be apt to specifically pinpoint and briefly discuss those factors that are said to have serious implication in human life.

Natural environment

A clean and pollution-free environment is very important for proper growth and development; a degraded environment (devoid of trees, plants, fauna and flora, rivers, canals, lakes, ponds, etc.) is injurious to man's health, growth and development. Man has begun to suffer growth hazards because he has made onslaughts on the environment, degrading it beyond repairs. We are growing physically weak day by day and becoming victim of several unheard kinds of diseases due to (a) increasing inactivity, and (b) degradation of natural environment. It is a known fact that inhabitants of hilly areas and those living in colder climates, where environment still is more natural and healthy, have better standards of health, longevity and growth than those living in degraded and unfavourable environment.

Malnutrition

Next to air and water, food is the major life-sustaining factor. A child born and brought up in abject poverty, and a mother living in a state of utter penury inevitably suffer from malnutrition because they cannot afford good diet. Due to this, the child may have no optimal growth and the mother may not bear healthy children. After genetic factors, malnutrition is the most serious factor responsible for ill-health and retarded growth of the people almost everywhere in the world irrespective of their caste, creed, religion or language. Well-nourished children may develop better both physically and mentally and realize their growth potential to the optimal level than those who have been kept deprived of good nutrition. Deficiency diseases occur squarely due to malnutrition, permitting no child to grow and develop qualitatively in various dimensions of personality. Not only physical diseases and ailments occur due to lack of proper nutrition but also child's development suffers badly and prospects of his self-actualization retard.

Insanitation

Insanitation is the greatest bane of the poverty-stricken localities as well as slum areas and sometime the effluent areas as well. By and large sanitation is a civic responsibility, but the individual and his family also have a significant role to play in it. Insanitation is often the breeding ground for microbes and through them hundreds of specified and unspecified diseases which impinge upon the growth potential of children. Where insanitation and disease are rampant, there children are bound to suffer from stunted growth and low quality development – both physical and mental.

Lack of Awareness and Information

Millions of children all over the world suffer from growth disorders and have stunted growth because their parents and elders are illiterate and least aware of the practicable principles of nutrition, cleanliness, sanitation and child rearing. They live in conditions of insanitation, filth and squalor and are least bothered about how children ought to be brought up, often leaving them to fend for themselves; they, perhaps, know only how to bear children like bugs and add to population explosion. In spite of so much knowledge and information flowing through electronic and print media, people refuse to learn the much needed lessons and help their children move on to the path of proper growth, progress and prosperity. They are unmindful of the way uncongenial environment is striking at the roots of their children's development.

Pollution

Pollution of all sorts (atmospheric, noise, water, air, chemical, etc.) has the most serious effect on the health, growth and development of the people irrespective of the fact where they live. Those who live in polluted atmosphere, consume polluted water (made impure, or unfit due to natural contaminants or subsoil impurities or man-made devices such industrial effluents), breathe polluted air (a result of industrial smoke, atmospheric dust, nuclear radiation, etc), bear the impact of honking horns of the road vehicles or trains, hi-fi loudspeakers, etc., have deleterious effects on the growth of their infants and children and the capacity of the older children to resist disease.

Customs and Traditions

Man's social growth and development - sometimes physical and mental aspects of growth also - are badly affected by customs and traditions of the family, community, religion or society in which one is born and brought up. Several *do's* and *don'ts* prescribed by customs and traditions allow little freedom to the children to do things in their own ways. This impinges upon their social and mental growth, and is quite true about more conservative and orthodox communities and religious-minded families, than those with a progressive outlook. Better social relationships and mental attitudes that are very important for the proper growth human personality are developed when children are not forced to stick to outdated and outmoded customs and traditions. Taboos on eating, visiting or inviting friends, wearing clothes, taking medicine, playing, exercising, and treating common ailments - all influence growth in one way or the other perceptibly or imperceptibly.

Psychological Factors

The most significant environmental factors that very adversely affect human growth and development are psychological in nature e.g. anxieties, tensions, frustrations, stresses and strains, generally popping up due to man's greed for becoming rich and more rich and pursuit of materialistic philosophy of life; the economic and social reasons being additional considerations. Children are often under too much stress because of the iron discipline at school, burdensome academic work and too few opportunities for free play - rather no time for play - at home. The career-conscious parents force their children to devote more and more time to studies, no matter how straining the whole exercise might be. This gives children no opportunity to release their pent-up energies, and so manage mental stress that strikes at the vitals of child's growth and development.

Decreasing Physical Activity

Apart from nutrition, physical exercise is an extremely important correlate of growth and development. Bookworms (too studious) and children with inaptitude for physical exercise often have no qualitative growth. Their body is less resistant to disease and their mental processes are less stable. There is enough scientific evidence to practically show that exercisers have better standards of over-all growth and development than non-exercisers. It is important to note that good nutrition will be of little consequence in the absence of physical activity which can be as mild as yoga, as fast as aerobics, or as vigorous as games and sports. Regular participation in physical activity workouts has a cleansing effect on the body, mind and spirit.

Protection from Disease

A child may be born naturally healthy and fit and may be destined to grow in a normal way but if he is not protected against diseases such as measles, small pox, diphtheria, polio, cerebral palsy, tuberculosis, etc., as now-a-days medical men advice, he is likely to fall prey to deadly diseases. Polio may maim a child for the whole life and retard his growth and development. Immunization against it is a must for fuller growth and development.

HEREDITY AND ENVIRONMENT

Man is a combined product of heredity (***Nature***) and environment (***Nurture***). It is impossible to *understand* an individual's personality and the process of his growth and development without referring to his *nature* (inherited parental and family characteristics; in other words, the quality of the stuff he is made of), and his *nurture* (environment, upbringing, rearing, nutrition, playmates, surroundings, etc.). Heredity is often compared to *seed* and environment to *soil, air, water, nourishment,* etc. No one can be brought into this world without seed (heredity) and no one can grow and develop to be an adult to perform duties of life without environment. Heredity and environment are complementary to each other; one carries no significance without the other.

What is man? Of what stuff he is made? How does a tiny dot-like seed grow into a highly complex and complicated thinking and performing machine? Why, though basically an animal, man differs from other organisms? Why, though similar in major physical characteristics, human beings differ from one another in almost every element of behaviour, personality and character? Why children of the same parents, even Siamese twins, have different temperaments, tastes and tendencies of behaviour? and scores of other questions cannot be addressed without a thorough understanding of people's heredity and environment. Exceptions and commonalities, generalities and individualities in growth and development are impossible to understand without reference to nature and nurture.

While heredity is an invisible force which guides the reproductive process and determines different traits and tendencies of behaviour that various organisms and animal species including humans shall have; environment comprises of all visible and invisible conditions, factors and forces that provide a climate to the organisms to grow and develop and express their *possibilities* in terms of traits, abilities, capacities, capabilities, etc. While heredity is a determining factor, environment is a modifying, motivating and inspiring force.

Heredity (genetic endowment) is a fixed element of human personality and growth in terms of its potential, environment is a very flexible, fluid and dynamic force. Heredity produces resemblances and dissimilarities both in

genotype (in the inherited traits) and ***phenotypes*** (in outward appearance, complexion and physical characteristics). Environment does nothing to alter or change a trait determined by heredity; it can facilitate or debilitate its development. Environmental modifications in inherited traits are rarely heard; they are negligible, so to say.

Whether great scientists, artists, musicians, writers, sportspersons, technocrats, military commanders, etc., are born or made, has always been a riddle, so difficult to solve. Knowledgeable people feel that individuals with rare qualities are born, environment only helps them grow and develop their potential. There is dearth of people who think otherwise and hold the contrary view; they believe that exceptional people are product of their environment (opportunities, interactions, conditions, situations, struggle, etc). Among a large number of students in a peer-group in a school, some children are intelligent, some dull and stupid; some are musical, some have no taste for music; some are studious, some athletic; and some extrovert, and some introvert. The same environment at school fails to make every child a leader, a scientist, a mathematician, an astronomer or a literary figure of some consequence. This shows that the real difference lies in not in nurture but in nature. As a fruit is sweet, sour or bitter due to its seed, not environment, so is an individual different from others due to their genetic make-up and upbringing.

Heredity

Heredity is nature's act of 'passing on of physical and mental characteristics genetically from one generation to another'. It is what we inherit biologically from our parents, grandparents, great grandparents and so on in the dynastic lineage. Peter Sandiford says:

> Heredity to some is a mysterious force which moulds off-spring in the likeness of parents, to others it is the antithesis of variation that is heredity consists in the resemblances, and in the dissimilarities between progenitors and descendents. Heredity is not force. Neither is it merely the likeness between offspring and parents; it includes all traits both like and unlike.

Put in a simple language, heredity is the potential each person receives from his or her parents through the transmission of genes. It is the sum-total of inborn traits, both similar and dissimilar, to those of the parents. With rare exceptions, most probably in case of monozygotic twins, every human being is genetically unique. Each of us shares traits with brothers, sisters, and parents, but none of us is exactly alike to any of them or any one else in the family. In the propagation of animal species, the invisible force that guides the reproductive process and determines each individual's characteristics, is, in terms of genetics, called heredity. Transmission of heredity characteristics from parents to children is not a mechanical process simply producing run-of the-mill individuals, exactly alike in structure and function, but a unique process governed by peculiar laws of nature determining both likeness and unlikeness. In nutshell, heredity is that imperceptible force which is at the root of resemblances and dissimilarities among parents and their progeny. It is an agent that demarcates the boundaries of one's physical growth and sets limits in terms of one's potential for overall potential.

Secrets of Heredity

As one candle lights another, so one life gives rise to another. A new life begins as a single cell - a fertilized ovum or female egg - technically known as *zygote,* which is created by the fusion of the spermatozoon (male sex cell) with the ovum. Heredity - the unique characteristics which each individual carries - is determined by a complex organization of chemical materials with the nucleus of the fertilized cell. The sperm, a stripped down cell shaped like a tadpole, is 3,00,000 times smaller than the ovum which is relatively enormous. It is one of the largest cells in the body - so large that can be visible to the naked eye. Although it weighs only a millionth of a gram, it contains considerable amount of cytoplasm and also a small amount of yolk needed to nourish the fertilized egg in its earliest days of growth. The female ovaries contain an estimated 4,00,000 eggs of which from 300 to 400 are released during a woman's fertility life. In this regard, the male partner of progeny has been so abundantly supplied with that one emission there are released 300 million to 500 million sperms to meet the egg to lay the foundation for a new life. The sex of the new child is determined right at the moment of the fertilization and is governed by nature's own laws governing genetics.

All cells in the human body except the sex cell - sperm or ovum - contain 46 chromosomes, a definite number of bodies, arranged in the nucleus in 23 pairs. Only sperm and egg contain 23 chromosomes each. Each female cell sex has identical chromosomes called XX, and each male sex cell carries XY chromosomes. When the two opposite cells fuse into one, the zygote contains 23 paired chromosomes. Chromosomes are strands of DNA (deoxyribonucleic acid). Along with some proteins, they also carry the vital genetic information in their basic functional units called genes. Genes are lined up on the chromosomes in the nucleus (the centre) of the sex cell. Some genes are dominant and some dormant.

Every individual in this world can be differentiated and identified at the molecular level on the basis of his or her DNA, the genetic material which it inherits from his biological parents, and which is identical in every cell. With the exception of identical twins, no human child has identical sequences. At the moment of conception, a sperm and an ovum, each containing half of each pair of the parent's chromosomes, combine to form a new individual and the chromosomes join to form new pairs. Though many people look alike and have common characteristics no two individuals, except identical twins, are exactly alike genetically.

The combination of good genes from both male and female parents makes really good heredity, while poor combination results in inferior inheritance. Genetic scientists believe that we do not, in fact, receive our bodies from our parents but only a germ-plasm - the seed, an aggregate of characteristics - which by some mysterious force transforms into a human being. Interestingly, the germ-cell which produces a dog may be similar to the one producing man yet the one gives rise to puppy, the other to a child. In 1875, Francis Galton had pointed out that the child, in a sense, is as old as the parent, indeed as old as the remotest parent; "the parent is rather the trustee of the germ-plasm than the producer of the child". The reproductive part of the germ-plasm is passed on from generation to generation as if withdrawn from one bank and deposited in another. The fusion of the material from the male and female parents seals the fate of the foetus by determining once for all its traits and characteristics it would exhibit as a human being. This means that one's heredity and the potential it carries is fixed at the time zygote comes into existence. Nothing, for sure, can be added or subtracted from it, and changed or modified later. Biologists have shown that genes create certain gross common features for all representatives of the *Homo Sapiens*. For example, they all have an upright posture, a pair of eyes and a pair of ears, a pair of arms and legs each, and they are bilaterally symmetrical. They have the same body chemistry and a capacity for feeling and thinking, for speaking, imagining, remembering and reproducing. Exceptions in such cases are rare. Our genetic heritage is unaffected by our day-to-day experiences and routine. It is noteworthy that due to physical and physiological adaptations to changing environmental conditions over tens of thousands of years, humans have evolved a highly organized social life that allows learning to influence their behaviour. Our brains act as libraries of information. Every new enriching experience affects our later behaviour. Proponents of nurture position, however, suggest that human beings are not limited by their genetic heritage because experience, training and a little hard work can stretch their potential to amazing lengths.

Though physical structure, size, colour, body chemistry, efficiency of physiological functioning, temperament, and even intelligence, to an extent, are a matter closely related to heredity, they too are influenced by external forces. Though the physical structure, size, complexion, colour of the eye, quality of hair on the body, the physiological capacity to function, temperament, intelligence, etc., to some extent, are inherited; they are influenced by environmental forces and factors. A person's genetic make-up is the foundation on which all his or her characteristics and behaviours are built. Experiences in the environment act in collaboration with the inheritance to shape day-today behaviour and patterns of development.

The three fundamental laws, which govern the mechanism of heredity include: (1) Like begets like (similar material produces similar material); (2) Like also produces unlike (similar material may produce dissimilar material); and (3) Law of regression. ***Like begets like*** means that a mango seed gives rise to a mango tree and not to an orange tree; and a dog produces a puppy, not a kitten; so human beings produce children who are like them in most respects. ***Like also produces unlike*** is a pointer to the fact that similarity tends to produce variation. Dark complexioned parents do have fair complexioned children and stupid parents may have intelligent children. In other words, we are not exactly like our parents. A hundred percent resemblance among parents and their children is impossible. Variation is not a haphazard process and governed by definite principles. The ***Law of Regression*** underlines the fact that the transmission of hereditary characteristics is never complete but partial; rather there is inevitably a tendency for various genetic traits/characteristics to move towards the centre or averages. Tall parents tend to have short children and dull parents tend to have bright children, and vice versa over generations. In aggregate their traits remain almost the same.

Environment

Environment consists of all external factors and forces – physical, social, ecological, economic, political and ideational – that potentially influence the quality, and direction of the development of personality and behaviours. It neither adds to nor subtracts anything from the hereditary material which gets transmitted from one generation to another, but has the capacity to afford any amount of opportunities to the people to self-actualize themselves within the limits and limitations imposed by nature on their potential. Stated in simple language, environment is simply a correlative of heredity; it merely determines which and to what extent, can heredity traits be developed. While heredity is considered as the fixed and non-modifiable component of human personality and behaviour, environment is dynamic, flexible and modifiable aggregate of hundreds of factors and forces that influence human growth and development. In the absence of environment, heredity is incapable of producing any offspring. The seed requires an environment to transform itself into a plant and bear fruit. This is true about animals and human beings alike.

From the viewpoint of growth, environment can be divided into prenatal (before birth) environment, and postnatal (after birth) environment. The ***prenatal environment*** has its own importance for the normal development can proceed only when the liquid which surrounds the growing foetus inside mother's womb has proper thermal and chemical properties. Added to it is the expectant mother's own state of body functions and mind. Compared to ***postnatal (external or after birth) environment***, the prenatal environment is constant, simple and limited in terms of time and space; nevertheless, the developing organism is susceptible to a variety of changing conditions within the mother including nutritional deficiencies, infections chemical changes in the maternal blood resulting from mother's emotional states, and exposure to radiation. There is a variety of implications and complications of the prenatal (internal) environment. In any case, the important of prenatal environment cannot be under-estimated thought the specific ways in which it influences later development of a child are largely unknown. The most obvious environmental influences are those which act upon the organism and the organism reacts to them after birth. As a child enters this world, he gets exposed to a complex external environment with its variety of physical, chemical and human energies, which influence his growth and development in thousand ways. This external environment, in our day-to-day terminology, is referred to 'environment', and is the most important factor in the growth and development of personality. The environment (external environment) is subdivided into (a) physical environment, and (b) social environment.

Physical environment refers to the physical and ecological surroundings such as vegetation, fauna & flora, rivers, landscape, mountains, hills, the sun, the air, the water, the buildings, roads, factories, industry, and so on. The geographical locale of place, climatic conditions, weather, seasons, etc., are important components of the external environment, and considered part and parcel of our existence. They affect our growth and development significantly. Our physical features and physiological functioning show clear traces of the influence of the environment we live in. The complexion, colour (of the skin, the hair), capacity for work, endurance, etc., of the people living in colder regions is significantly different from that of those living in hot climates. Living and working conditions of a place have a great impact on the development of certain abilities. Biologically, either the organisms adapt to the environmental conditions or face the extinction threat. Human beings not only adapt to the environment but also have the capacity to alter their environment within the limits and limitations of their power. With his intelligence, man has been making all efforts to make the environment more conducive to the growth of his self and the society.

Social environment consists of people and their ideas, beliefs, thoughts, experiences, convictions, prides, prejudices, customs, traditions, laws, rules, regulations, and so on. With the growth of mind and intelligence in man, the social environment has changed dramatically over the last ten thousand years. More changes are sweeping fast over the horizons. Man's growth, development, behaviour and performance in all fields of interaction and knowledge bear the impress of his culture especially that of ethics, philosophy, economics, etc. The human behaviour is increasingly becoming more complex and complicated because of the social ecology is undergoing inevitable and irreversible change. The swift means of transport and communication, the irresistible electronic media, and the push-button culture have put the well-established values of life under severe strain. Both the inherited and the acquired behaviour are being subjected to tremendous pressure of change with unexpected consequences for the humanity as a whole. The pursuit of materialistic philosophy with increasing consumerism all around has brought qualitative change in man's life-style. Man' affiliation and affinity with nature have been gradually receding farther and still farther.

All environmental forces are external, and least constant and controllable. They possess tremendous potential to influence human development and determine its direction. They too have limitations when considered against the forces of nature; for instance, they are incapable of changing the basic hereditary characteristics. Social interaction, varied experiences of man, training and education - all environmental factors - are so dynamic and powerful that they can modify anything to some extent by way of compensatory mechanism. However, it is still a mystery as to how qualitatively these factors individually or collectively can influence the development of hereditary characteristics and to what extent. Apart from this, no two human beings have exactly the same environment since they cannot be exactly at the same place at the same time. Geographically and socially, it might look the same for the time being, but not always, but from the viewpoint of effects of environment on their personal development, things will always be different. For example, in a family with two sons, and child has older brother and other a younger brother, and the parents may treat the older and the younger children quite differently. Apart from this, these children will have different friends, and will be liable to develop different interests, skills, aptitudes, and attitudes. Later they might identify themselves with different religious, political, social, and athletic groups and organizations. A single environmental factor, sometimes seemingly insignificant, is capable of giving different direction to a person's behaviour, character and personality. Depending upon how the genetic material reacts and interacts with such a factor, the pendulum of result can sway to positive or negative side. That is why it not possible, nor can it be wise to attach some sort of certainty to the extent of human development on the basis of either genetic potential or environmental factors. Stretched to an extreme point, the impact of environment on certain variables of growth, development or behaviour may be felt in a single generation or in a single individual, but the consequent change whatsoever cannot be permanent and observed in the succeeding generations because this is an acquired modification. Environment is simply a correlative of heredity helping the latter to develop its potential to its fullest extent. Education and training do influence behaviour a lot within their respective limits and limitations; they cannot change the basic quality of the traits inherited by an individual.

GROWTH AND DEVELOPMENT: GENETIC AND ENVIRONMENTAL EFFECTS

No efforts of the scientists, educationists, psychologists or others till date have been able to convince people as to the greater importance of heredity or environment in the growth, development and determination of the behaviour of a child. The opinion is still divided on the magnitude of the role of the two in the growth and development of an individual as a unique personality.

The two schools of thought (holding heredity position and environment position) have diametrically opposite views on the issue. The school led by Rousseau, Francis Galton, Pearson, Dugdale, Goddard and others value heredity higher than environment in determining the quality of growth and development and, so the kind of personality a person shall have in life. According to this school, human potential for development of various characteristics and abilities is generally determined at the time of conception and is, more or less, fixed;

nothing can be added to or subtracted from it later. Hundreds of genetic studies conducted on identical twins and fraternal twins are often cited to prove the higher value of heredity in human growth and development.

The environment-position-holding school pioneered by Candole of France, Howard. John Locke, and others place greater confidence in environment than on heredity as determinant of growth and development and personality. The architects of this school believe that environment can mould, change and alter even the basic genetic material (hereditary characteristics). The experiments of Newman, Freeman and Holzinger on identical twins are cited as strong proof in favour of environment as the anchor of child's growth and development. Skodak also tried to prove this point with the help of his studies on the intelligence of the original mothers of some children.

Despite convincing arguments and evidence in favour of the two view-points, the needle of the judgment points towards the centre, showing that the neither school is totality correct nor totally wrong in their respective assumptions. In fact, the importance of both heredity and environment in human growth and development is now well-recognized irrespective of the percentage of share either contributes.

A few important facts will suffice to make the haze clear from the effects heredity and environment make on growth and development.

- Importantly, growth and development is a very comprehensive process. It is absurd to put it in watertight physical, mental, intellectual and social compartments. To have a holistic view of growth is important. A physically weak poor boy (due to malnutrition or underfeeding) may be top in his mathematics class, and a physically strong and well-built boy may be as dull as a stone in class work but a genius in a sport. One aspect of growth cannot be isolated from the other(s).

- While the hard core heredity-position holding scientists are not ready to accord place of importance to environment in the scheme of things in human growth and development, the staunch environment-position holders stick to their view-point considering it superior and superb in comparison to the other. The evidence pertaining to their relative importance is almost equal. No organism can be produced and reared singularly either by heredity or environment.
- Heredity and environment are not isolates but correlates of each other; one can do nothing without the other. Without seed there cannot be fruit, nor can a plant bear fruit without air, water, good soil, manure, protection from disease, etc. No seed can grow into a plant unless it is sown in good soil, watered well, given proper and timely manure, and nourished well.
- There is a general consensus among scientists that no feature or characteristic of a child is due exclusively to hereditary, nor exclusively due to environment. A child may have the potential to grow into a perfectly healthy and strong person to become an athlete in due course but this may not happen unless he is able to live in a favourable environment, acquire needed skills, practice the sport to the point of perfection, and compete in well-structured athletic competitions. This is what makes environment as complex and mysterious as heredity.
- No one can say that blue eyes are inherited but a brown skin is acquired, because the nutrition in childhood and climate all through may mould or alter the basic potential for these traits. It also cannot be concluded that a dog's bark is inherited but his response to his name is learnt. Reared in isolation a dog may fail to bark and unless an inherent teach-ability exists no dog will learn to come when called. Similarly a child may have inherited the native

equipment of intelligence - a complex memory system, a very sensitive nervous system and a superior brain - but he will neither learn language nor skills nor etiquettes nor manners nor any other social attribute unless the environment is facilitating for development of the characteristics associated with these abilities.

- A person may have inherited a strong and tall skeletal structure from his family but if the environment denies him good nutrition, protection from disease, health care, pollution-free atmosphere, opportunity for exercise, etc., his growth and development will surely suffer and he may not be able to realize his full potential and make use of inherited quality in developing into a basketball or volleyball player.
- Instances are there of the children with poor genetic background becoming physically strong and mentally sharp because they could manage to live in a better environment. With adapted teaching methods, specialized equipment and learning aids even the mentally challenged children have been able to achieve incredible standards of growth and development and success in life.
- It is impossible to predict the quality of growth and development of an individual because (1) we do not exactly know what his growth potential is except that his family history has not been too bad; (2) what sort of environment he has encountered at various stages of his growth; (3) we also are not sure of the kind and quality of interaction between his heredity and the environment; and (4) how heredity and environment will get locked in a struggle for supremacy and with what effects.
- If a child is born in a family of well-learned and intelligent people, and if the child has no aptitude for studies, he may remain inferior to his stock. On other hand, a child born in a poor and illiterate

family but surrounded by a good society right from the beginning, is likely to achieve better standards of mental growth and development than other members of his family have been able to.

- The *principle of compensation* states that you can make up your deficiency in one aspect by doing better in another. For example, if a child received poor genetic material in terms of intelligence, he can make up the deficiency by working very hard over time on tasks that contribute to intelligence. Children with inborn high intelligence may get at the things just with a little hard work. A girl may achieve high ranking in studies because she is studious and works very hard; on the other hand, a boy may achieve the same status by comparatively little hard work because he is basically genius and has the ability to solve problem in a twinkle.
- Effects of heredity and environment on human growth and development - whether physical, mental, intellectual or social - are relative and cannot be measured using absolute norms and standards. Moreover, there are no appropriate yardsticks available to evaluate the effects of the two complex forces of nature in objective ways.

QUESTIONS FOR EXERCISE

Short-answer Questions

Keeping answered short-questions at the end of Chapter-I, answer the following questions as precisely as possible:

1. Name the important sciences from which physical education receives its theoretical framework.
2. What changes, according to Charles Darwin, have occurred in the structure and features of man during the Evolutionary Process?
3. List out the major factors assisted the transition from ape to man.

4. What consequential changes occurred in man due to his adapting the upright posture?
5. For what did man use his muscle during his history of evolution?
6. Define growth and development in simple words.
7. Differentiate between growth and development.
8. Explain how growth is a quantitative and development qualitative.
9. Why growth and development, as biological terms, are used in conjunction with each other and not separately?
10. List the hereditary factors that affect human growth.
11. How does malnutrition adversely affect human growth?
12. Briefly describe the psychological factors which badly affect human development.
13. Enumerate some basic facts about heredity.
14. Highlight the secrets of heredity.
15. What is germ-plasm and how does it affect human growth and development?
16. Briefly explain the three laws of heredity.
17. Define environment in your own words.
18. Describe the components of social environment.
19. How does social environment affect a child's growth?
20. Briefly describe the effects of heredity on a child's growth.
21. What is the general consensus among scientists about heredity and environment?
22. What is the stand of heredity-position holders on human personality?
23. Explain the principle of compensation in traits.
24. Justify heredity being called a mysterious force.
25. Explain whether outstanding athletes are born or made.

CHAPTER: FOUR

PSYCHOLOGICAL BASIS OF PHYSICAL EDUCATION

According to natural scientists human beings can be distinguished from animals on the basis of three major characteristics: (1) *an upright posture* (standing erect and walking on two limbs rather than fours, as mammals do); (2) *an opposable thumb* (thumb of the human hand is very versatile; it can touch all fingers); and (3) ***a complex nervous system and superior brain*** (the thinking, memorizing and analyzing cerebral cortex). The upright posture gave man not only a distinct look but also facilitated a varied range of mobility in his upper limbs resulting in the capacity to acquire an endless variety of skills and abilities which no other animal species could have. The opposable thumb made man really an artist and a technician who could create and assimilate unique skills of writing, painting, wielding and using a variety of instruments and implements, which enabled him to usher an era of civilization. The development of a complex nervous system and a superior brain in the form of cerebral cortex transformed man-the-animal into a thinking living engine – a status, which no other animal has ever deserved. We are well aware how these biological changes in structure and function enabled man to usher in *Cultural Revolution.*

From the psychologists' point of view, human beings are "biological animals who think and behave within a social environment". This statement carries three significant facts:

- Being biological animals, human beings share a common evolutionary history with other organisms, as result of which the tendencies of their behaviour are no different from those of animals. Instincts expressed in emotions are still a dominating force in man's behaviour even though man has learnt to be no slave to his instincts.

- Human beings are thinking animals because they possess the native equipment of perception, thought and cognition (the cerebrum in addition to the primitive brains of the animals). They experience and can store experiences, and retrieve them from the memory store as and when needed. In this respect animals and human beings have no parallel.
- Behaviour – activity of organism's body and mind – occurs productively only in a social environment; in other words, human beings interact within the social environment, the physical environment acts just as a backdrop.

The existence of mind gives man a special status among the biological animals and also adds a new dimension to his personality and a new meaning to his being. Mind is of utmost importance in explaining human behaviour that has at least four major aspects: physical, mental, emotional and social. No physical activity of man can be understood, discussed and analyzed without reference to such mental functions as sensation, perception, memory, response and feedback. It is here we find physical education having its roots embedded in psychology, which is a study of behaviour. The relationship between physical education and psychology is very close; rather it can be said that physical education without psychology is like a body without soul.

PSYCHOLOGY

During the evolutionary process, as human intelligence grew, man became curious about the universe of things around him. It was natural for him to look around and to know how events occur the way they do. In the beginning, man's curiosity and his inquiry into the nature of things were concentrated on concrete things. Gradually, with learning and education coming up fast, the focus shifted to abstract phenomenon like soul, mind, spirit, etc. This resulted into the birth of philosophy which in its simplest form is known as *love of wisdom* with its focus on soul (i.e. the *quality of thought*). In ancient days, there was no psychology but every thing concerning soul came under philosophy. Since the *soul* was studied and discussed in philosophy in details, more scientific-minded thinkers considered it worthwhile to call this new branch of philosophy as the study of mind with stress on how thought is produced and not what thought is. So from the universe of philosophy emerged psychology, focusing on more concrete aspect of so-called soul. The problem was not yet over because like soul, mind also could not be observed concretely. Today, psychology is much more than simply a study of soul or mind of the ancient times; it encompasses several areas of knowledge including physiology, neuroscience, information processing, etc.

Meaning and Definition of Psychology

Psychology is said to have originated from two Greek words - *psyche* (meaning soul) and *logos* (meaning to talk about or science). Being a part of philosophy, psychology in ancient times was considered as the *study of the soul.* Long after the vague ideas of Greek philosophers about psychology, in 1590 A.D., Rudolf Geockel, for the first time, used the word psychology meaning *study of the mind.* Because mind, an abstract notion, was difficult to locate in the body, some people started calling psychology as the *study of consciousness.* It was Sigmund Freud and his associates who found that the mind also worked at subconscious and unconscious levels, so, for them, it was wrong to label psychology as study of consciousness only. Freud believed that the mind expressed itself in behaviour. Therefore, with Freudians and Behaviourists psychology came to be better understood as the *study of behaviour.*

Psychology may or may not be accepted today as a study of soul or mind, or consciousness but none of these concepts can be overlooked while considering psychology as the study of behaviour. There can be no behaviour without reference to mind and consciousness. William McDougall (1949) called psychology as "a science which aims to give us better understanding and control of the behaviour of the organism as a whole." Modern psychologists, therefore, attempt to understand, to get an insight into, to interpret, and throw light on the mental processes and the behaviour resulting there from. In the study of behaviour, Woodworth attached great importance to the individual's heredity and his environment. He, therefore, called psychology as the *science of activities of an individual (organism) in relation to his environment.*

Psychology, now-a-days, is "the scientific study of behaviour and mental processes of humans and other animals". It is rightly stated that mind is the central notion of psychology and behaviour is the expression of mind and is also the subject of its study. This means, where there is behaviour, there psychology is involved directly or indirectly. It is impossible to study behaviour without using scientific method. In the eyes of the modern psychologists, psychology is a science which investigates all kinds of behaviour in whatever settings or environments it occurs. That is why psychology has several branches viz. Educational Psychology, Child Psychology, Clinical Psychology, Medical Psychology, Criminal Psychology, Physiological Psychology, Individual Psychology, Industrial Psychology, Social Psychology, Sport Psychology, and so on, each branch dealing with a specific branch dealing with specific type of behaviour in a specific setting with a specific purpose in view.

From the different definitions of psychology, it could be concluded that:

1. Psychology is essentially the study of behaviour - animal as well as human.
2. The concept of mind is basic to psychology. No discussion on psychology is complete without reference to mind and its processes.
3. Psychology has now become a science because it uses scientific tools and techniques to understand and deal with behaviour.

4. Environment plays a crucial role in shaping human behaviour because it programmes the software of man's mind in childhood.

SPORTS PSCYHOLOGY

Sport as a recreation is for every one but sport as competition, is for a talented few. Most people love to watch others playing sports; they enjoy sport as spectators. The last 50 years have seen sports emerging as a great socio-cultural force influencing human behaviour all over the world. People engage in sports activity in a variety of ways - as athletes, as trainers, as scientists (researchers, doctors, physiotherapists), as organizers, as administrators, as game officials (judges, referees, umpires, jury, officials, etc.) and as spectators. Where there is man, there is sport behaviour; and where there is behaviour, involving both body and mind, there is bound to be sport psychology - the study of sport behaviour.

Athletes give out outstanding performances not simply due to their hard physical training effort and instruction from their trainers but also due to the active part played by scientists who generally remain in the background. Today, no young talented kid can be groomed into a star performer without assistance from different branches of science such as physiology, biomechanics, psychology, nutrition, health sciences, etc. From a simple child-play, generally called motor-skill acquisition phase, to performing at the Olympic Games and winning *Gold*, is a result of the inter-play of innumerable visible and invisible factors and forces that influence training human muscle and mind over time for such unique endeavours. Experts in sports training methodology consider three sports sciences viz. physiology, biomechanics, and psychology of critical importance in the preparation of athletes for top performances. Physiology develops the energy basis, biomechanics helps improve mechanical skills and psychology is the ultimate determining (mind) factor in winning a game.

Meaning and Definition of Sport Psychology

The world psychology, says Bryant Cratty, refers to the study of human behaviour and sport psychology as a branch (or subcategory) of psychology focusing on athletes. The athletes and athletic trainers are today convinced that there could be no excellence in sport without scientific backup, and that a game is won in the mind before it is won physically. That is why, along with biomechanics and physiology, sport psychology is considered as a critical sport science. ***The branch of psychology that deals with the behaviour of sportspersons in learning, practice and competitive situations with a view to improve performance is called sport psychology.*** This is an emerging science that makes possible "the application of psychological principles to sport and physical activity at all levels of skill improvement," said Margaret Brown & Michael Mahoney. Much of the subject matter of sport psychology is of practical nature perused by physical education teachers, coaches and athletes. According to Professor Robert N. Singer – the former president of the International Society of Sport Psychology - sport psychology is "***associated with understanding, explaining, and influencing selected behaviors of individuals and groups involved in high level sport, recreation sport, exercise, and other vigorous activities***". In an early statement, Singer had explained the nature, content and objectives of sport psychology as under:

> Sport psychology is an applied psychology in the same way military and industrial psychologies are. It encompasses of various branches of psychology as they are related to our ability to understand athletic performance, how to make it better, and how to influence favorable psychological outcomes from experiences in sport and exercise program.

With the craze and quest for the Olympic gold medals increasing at tremendous rate in these years in the athletes and their nations, sport psychology is being defined "as a science in which the principles of psychology are applied in sport setting". These principles are often applied to enhance athletes' performance. Some sport psychologists go beyond this objective of sport psychology, and along with this they place equal emphasis on the enrichment of social-psychological aspects of human life. Even in physical education and sport people study behaviour from various angles and for various objectives e.g. play therapy, skill-acquisition, physical exercise therapy, etc. But sport psychologists as such bring their efforts to bear on the competitive athletes, the social dynamics of the team, and the environmental forces including sports fans and spectators.

From various definitions cited above, the following salient features of sport psychology emerge:

- Sport psychology is a unique branch of psychology.
- Several branches of psychology (especially educational psychology, experimental psychology, clinical psychology) contribute to the making of its body of knowledge.
- Sport psychology deals with all types of athletic behaviour.
- Its major aim is to help the athletes at all levels of practice and competition to improve their performance.
- It is rightly called as 'a legitimate branch of sports medicine'.

Since increasing stress is being laid on the improvement of performance in sport, sport psychologists, in cooperation with the physiologists and sports coaches, are constantly in look out for new techniques of *preparing, training and conditioning* mind and providing intervention to the athletes to that effect so that they perform at their best and ward off negative effects of competitive situations on their body and mind and even giving interventions to the sportspersons so that they can give out their best. Sport psychology is now understood to be the ultimate hope for the performing athletes.

MEANING AND DEFINITION OF PERSONALITY

We all have a personality that makes us different from every one else. Each one of us has a unique physical frame, features and qualities of mind and heart. Sometimes a child resembles his brother or sister a great deal and yet in many ways he/she is different from them. Such statements as "Jawaharlal Nehru was a great personality"; "My Hindi teacher has a poor personality"; and "Ram Khilavan, the gardener of our school, hardly possesses any personality" speak volumes about the individuals referred to in these statements and also the understanding and attitude of the statement makers towards these persons. For example, 'Jawaharlal Nehru was a great personality' might mean that he was born of a high family; had held the highest position of leadership in the country; was a great world statesman and a writer, so on and so forth; that is why he was a great personality. The Hindi teacher has a short weak skeletal frame; is very soft-spoken, meek and humble; is not aggressive and assertive; so he is a poor, an unimpressive personality. The school gardener is an underdog; he often puts on dirty clothes; remains soiled the whole day; enjoys no nutritious diet; often suffers from variety of illnesses and diseases; is totally illiterate and his routines are no better than of a domestic animal; he is least concerned with world beyond his nose; therefore, he seemingly has ***no*** personality.

For a common man a good personality means a big, awesome and impressive physical structure - the bigger the stature, better the personality; shorter or frailer the physical frame, poorer the personality. It is so because the first impression a person casts on others is that of his appearance (or profile) – his body and its dimensions, his dress, footwear, the way he dresses up and the like; rest of the aspects such as intellect, mental soundness, social relationships, etc., come later and are less observable at first sight than the physical dimensions. It was utterly wrong on the part of some people to consider Prime Minister Lal Bahadur Shatri – the man with a short stature – a poor personality. The towering intellect, firm determination and confidence with which he was successful in winning the Indo-Pak War in 1965, were simply superb and tell a lot about his real *self*, and the self is much more than merely the body. The self has physical, mental, intellectual, emotional and social dimensions. That is, perhaps, why the concept of personality is still vague and differs from person to person.

Tertiary Meaning of Personality and Personality Quotes

The word personality is derived from *persona*, originally meaning "theatrical mask" worn by dramatis personae (actors) in a play to depict á particular actor such as devil, an animal or a saint. Carl Jung - a famous disciple of Sigmund Freud - used this word in connection with his theory of self (personality) which plays several social roles given to the individual by the society. Since those times, there has been dramatic change in the concept and definition of personality. Some authors defined personality as "pattern of behaviour in a certain way" or simply "intelligence of mind" or "a man's ways of being, acting, reacting and interacting". The notion about personality has always been dynamic; it could neither be fixed, nor unchangeable. As we find life in several forms, so do we find personality in hundreds of hues and colours.

Psychologists have no agreement on the definition of personality. Therefore, personality has been defined in a variety of ways. Morton Prince considered personality as "the sum total of all the biological innate dispositions, impulses, tendencies, appetites and instincts of the individual and the dispositions and tendencies acquired by experience." John Watson - the leader of the Behaviourist School - defined personality as "the sum of activities that can be discovered over a long enough period of time to give reliable information." With Norman Cannon, personality is the "dynamic organization of interlocking behaviour systems that each of us possesses, as he grows from a biological new born to a biosocial adult in an environment of other individuals and cultured products." William James found personality "consisting of layers viewed from within which he called self. In sequence, they are: the *individual self* (body, possessions, family, friends, etc.) *social self, spiritual self* and *pure ego*". In Carl Pearson's views, personality "is the effect upon others of a living being's appearance, and behavior so far as they are interpreted as distinctive signs of that being."

Eysenck looked at personality as "more or less stable and enduring organization of a person's character, temperament, intellect, and physique, which determines his unique adjustment to the environment." Gordon Allport proclaimed: "Personality is a dynamic organization within the individual of those psychophysical systems that determine his unique adjustment to his environment."

Guilford believed that the individual personality, with all its uniqueness, surfaces from out of the individual differences that exist. For him, personality is "an individual unique pattern of traits". Maddi found a wider perspective of personality, which, he says, "is a stable set of characteristics and tendencies that determine those commonalities and differences that have continuity in time and that may or may not be easily understood in terms of the social and biological pressure of the immediate situation alone." Dr. Radhakrishnan – the great Indian philosopher – remarked: "Personality is the union of our acts and potentialities, a complex unit of body, mind and spirit. It is the symbol of human unity in the midst of incessant flow." Walter Mischel – a noted personality theorist – argues: "Personality usually refers to the distinctive patterns of behaviour (including thoughts and emotions) that characterize individual's adaptation to the situations of his or her life." It may also be defined as "a particular pattern of behaviour and thinking prevailing across time and situations that differentiate one individual from another."

While defining personality, the early psychologists placed greater emphasis on inherited characteristics (fixed and rigid raw material such as physique, temperament, intelligence, etc.), the modern psychologists consider "individual-environment interaction" as the more powerful determinant of personality than inborn traits. The three-fold conception of man as body, mind and spirit points to an important truth that man is not a mere object, his spiritual nature gives him a very unique position in the universe, and his soul and body can participate in a new order of spirit and existence. The dynamic self of man is always interacting, adapting, adjusting, assimilating and integrating.

More and more psychologists have begun to believe that the real personality of an individual emerges from interaction between the heredity (seed) and the environment (external factors and forces). It is totality wrong to say that a child inherits his personality from his parents and grandparents; in fact, he only receives the germ-plasm which flourishes into a personality only after it struggles against the forces of environment. Scientists may be able to study and account for common characteristics found among people but they cannot explain why an individual is different from every other individual - even his sisters and brothers. There is no objective yardstick under the sun which can assess uniqueness every one of us possesses. It is, therefore, difficult to define personality in absolute terms and words which cover all unique individuals.

A few most important ***key concepts*** inherent in the definitions of personality quoted above may be summed up as under:

- Personality is ***a dynamic concept***. It can not be confined to certain inherited traits (thoughts, intelligence), tendencies and behaviours.
- The inner aspect of personality comprises of inherited characteristics, qualities, features, traits etc. Its outer aspect is seen in individual differences among people.
- No single definition can define personality so that it covers all that every individual is made of.
- Despite physical, mental, intellectual, social, spiritual and emotional dimensions which personality has, there is integration, a unifying thread, putting them together.
- Without sustained interaction between genetic material and environmental factors, there can be no unique personality.
- Personality is what a person really is regardless of the way people perceive his qualities or the techniques/ methods with which psychologists study him.

- Personality evolves gradually as behavioural transformations occur as a result of individual-environment interaction.

PSYCHOLOGICAL FACTORS AFFECTING PHYSICAL PERFORMANCE

Most people now-a-days recognize that modern sport is more than muscle strength and ability for oxygen intake. Psychological traits and abilities play a significant role, particularly in competitive sports. An athlete may judge himself to be in the best of his physical condition (fitness-wise) and perfect in the skills and strategies of the game/event and yet give out an increasingly bad performance. Hundreds of examples can be quoted from every day sport scene to show that there is something beyond the physical domain that plays a crucial part in determining an athlete's success at the competition. A disastrous performance on one occasion may convince an athlete that he lost because there was something wrong with his *mind* though bodily he was in a perfect *fighting fit* condition.

Athletic performance in an elite or top sport is not simply due to an athlete's or team's behaviour/actions (efforts, play styles, strategies, tactics, etc.) during a particular competition, but it is the result of a long period of training and exposure in competitive situations, which involve both physical and psychological aspects. It is no use training body unless the mind is also trained simultaneously. Though body and mind are no separate entities, yet to achieve a top performance in sport with physiological and psychological components, body and mind have to function as a well-synchronized unit. The conditioning of physical factors such as strength, endurance with aerobic and anaerobic capacities, power and flexibility for performance-enhancement is fundamentally important and well known as they are explained in coaching theory. The training of mental faculties for elite performance is now gaining ground in the systems of sports training.

It is often observed that sportspersons are *over-educated* on physical factors and *under-educated* on mental factors. Obviously, too many athletes and their trainers still try hard to develop the human capacity for performance only by putting too much stress on physical conditioning, which now is proving to be totally wrong and inconsistent with the fact that human beings are units of body and mind and both must go hand-in-hand in building up an athlete's performance capacity.

Even if an athlete has prepared himself for the competition to the best of his ability both physically and mentally, there are hundreds of personal and environmental conditions, factors and forces that influence his performance and put hurdles on the road to his becoming a champion, for example, his emotions, mood states and attitudes. With the help of his trainer, an athlete may be able to take care of the physical parameters and personal factors so crucial to his performance, it is a Herculean task for him to control environmental influences except that he has to acquire the skills and strategies to combat some and manage others.

Psychological Factors affecting Physical Performance and their Implication in Sportsperson's Success

Since physical performance in any endeavour or enterprise, much less in sports, is a combined result of physical, psychological and environmental factors and forces, it is often difficult to pin-point exactly as to which factor is more crucial for impeding performance and to what extent. Physical factors are observable, so are several environmental factors; their influence can easily be pin-pointed. Most psychological factors influencing performance in all activities and sports are implicit and take long time before an athlete can learn how to understand, assess, control and manage them.

An analysis of the situation, points out the finger towards following psychological factors that affect performance both positively and negatively. These factors can be influenced and modified by applying various techniques and strategies.

1. Attitudes
2. Expectations
3. Tensions
4. Anxieties
5. Confidence
6. Over emotional-arousal
7. Concentration (Distraction)
8. Motivation
9. Mental training
10. Spectator influence

Attitudes

An attitude is a *stance, posture* or *position* an individual assumes about an object, a person or an event. Attitudes of the parents towards their children and vice versa, coach's attitudes towards his athletes and vice versa and our attitude towards life and life activities are well recognized. An attitude involves some sort of feeling or emotion and goes a long way in influencing our relationships with people and our efforts to make necessary adjustment in life. Athletes' attitudes towards the trainers, training regimens (workloads), competition, teammates, opponents, game officials, administrators, competition organizers, etc., have a power influence on his performance. Favourable attitudes produce favourable results and assist the process of performance-enhancement, while unfavourable attitudes (indifference) may impede performance. A belligerent attitude in a game often leads to brawls, quarrels and scuffles among the opponents, arousal of emotions and physical fighting, thereby badly influencing performance. Athlete's good attitude towards his coach and the workouts prescribed by him help the athlete give out best performance.

Expectations

Expectations play an important role in human life; they play equally significant role in athletic performance. When an athlete prepares for a competition intelligently, honestly and vigorously, he nurses great expectations to win. If unfortunately his expectations do not come true because something wrong goes somewhere, it leads to frustration affecting his future performance unless his approach is down-to-earth. Expectations are fine because they energize effort but over-expectations make the athlete unrealistic in his approach towards his abilities and his athletic exploits. Psychologists rightly advise the athletes that their *level of aspiration* and level of achievement must be congruent. The sportspersons must learn to train their minds in such a way that the result of their planning, preparation and participation in athletic competitions turn out to be directly proportional to the efforts put in. Unrealistic athletes keep their expectations too high unmindful of their capacities, the training inputs, with the result that they ultimately go to or hit the wall and their performance ends up in a disaster.

Tensions

Practice and competition of sport generates high levels of tension – both physical and mental. Physical tension results from hard workouts, over-practice, accidents, injury, discomfort and frustration on account of repeated failure. Mental tensions arise from too high stress on athlete's mind. Basically some sort of stress is necessary for the athletes to perform at an optimal level but too high stress arising from such environmental factors as bad play field conditions, unsuitable equipment, mismatching of the competitors, unfavourable competition fixtures, partiality on the part of the game officials, competition fever (especially for the young and inexperienced athletes), unfavourable spectators, coach's uncalled for interference in the team composition and dynamics at crucial moments etc. The stress response produces (a) *effects on our muscles* (discomfort or pain, trembling, restlessness, inability tot relax, tension); (b) *effects of the automatic nervous system* (sweating, dry mouth, pounding heart, feeling faint, tingling on the hands and feet, frequent urination); and (c) *effects of increased alertness of the mind* (fear, worry, distractibility, poor concentration, difficulty in sleeping, negative thoughts, etc.)

The older and more experienced athletes know how to manage stress and deal with the impinging factors but novices and junior athletes generally have tough time in managing stresses and releasing their tensions. Athletes use a variety of relaxation techniques such as yogic relaxation, Jacobson's muscular relaxation, meditation, pep-talks, hot baths, desensitization, imagery, behavioural modification, etc., to manage their stress and tensions arising out of competitive endeavours.

Anxieties

Called as a "disturbed state" of body and mind or a state of "nervousness", anxiety is apprehension of danger accompanied by restlessness and oppression in the digestive tract and viscera. It is generally caused by irrational fears. Psychologists categorize anxiety into *trait anxiety* and *state anxiety* – the one being an enduring characteristic of individual's personality, and the other a transitory state. This means that a person may be anxious by nature (inherited tendency to feel afraid) or he may encounter situations which arouse anxiety (for example, the presence of a cat in the room). Performing athletes face anxiety in hundred ways *before competition* (whether one would be selected on the team, who would play whom, under what conditions, etc, such thoughts create anxiety), *during competition* (situations like tough and tricky opponents, shoots at the goal going waste, team cohesion going hay wires, bad playing form, frequent warning from the referee, etc., cause anxiety) and even *after competition* (what will happen in next competition).

Anxiety affects man's psychological and physiological functions. For example, anxiety arouses a player to such an extent that he finds it hard to concentrate on his game and feel lost. Player's ability to judge things gets diminished and he cannot process much information; he intends to do one thing but does another – an unspecified one. The anxious athletes are generally tense as a result their ability to perform in tasks involving neuromuscular coordination deteriorates steeply. It is experimentally proved that anxiety impedes muscular performance, over-anxiety cripples it absolutely.

Psychologists suggest several strategies for the athletes to manage anxiety; they include muscular and mental relaxation, meditation, behavioural modification, visualization, imagery skill training, goal-setting, positive self-talk and the like.

Confidence

A confident athlete makes determined effort to win the game, and he often is a success. On the other hand, the one who lacks confidence gets defeated much before he enters the arena for a fight. A confident athlete dominates the proceedings while the confidence-shaky athlete looks for an excuse to run away from the battle field and often misplaces blame. Confidence is, in fact, built up in athletes by the team management (coach, manager, doctor and/or physiotherapist) by eliminating the causes that make an athlete lose heart; this may include poor skill level, lack of required physical fitness, inadequate practice, paucity of mental strength to face challenges, non-availability of standard equipment, little or no scientific backup, inadequate exposure in competitive situation, and so on.

Confidence building measures include striving for a perfect skill level, practice of the skills and game to the point of perfection, intrinsic and extrinsic motivation from the team management, ideal or near-ideal playing conditions, good inter-personnel relationships among players, encouragement, independent decision-making, minimal interference by the coach or any other official in athlete affairs, etc.

Over Emotional Arousal

As over-anxiety has crippling effect on the physical performance, so has the over emotional arousal. In order to recharge the energy batteries of their athletes, the team management (particularly coaches) arouses the players emotionally to unimaginable pitch as a result of which players become over-aggressive both on and off the field, endangering the safety of the opponents, that of their teammates, and their own. They use illegal tactics to subdue the opponents and intimidate game officials, which invariably lands them in trouble with the competition officials who take recourse to send-offs or severe warnings. It is important that the players must be trained to discipline their emotions and not permit them to soar high to controllable horizons. No doubt, players should be emotionally involved in the game but crossing the limits of decency in emotional arousal tells upon their health as well as performance; it deteriorates it beyond repairs. Unless checked by using cognitive therapy, behavioural modification strategies, frequent emotional arousal develops into a habitual behaviour and becomes detrimental to athletic performance.

Concentration

No game can be won without utmost concentration. All sportspersons invariably have to be focused in order to achieve best results. Sports like archery, shooting, fencing, diving, gymnastics, wrestling, boxing, judo, etc., need utmost concentration on the part of the players. The attention distracting factors are either personal (disturbed state of mind due to some personal shock, trauma, injury or physical discomfort) or environmental (such as undue interference by the team officials, bad relationship among team mates, unsuitable equipment, audience's unfavourable behaviour, uncertain weather conditions, badly maintained play fields, etc). A distracted athlete cannot perform creditably; rather it is difficult for him or her to sustain in the field. Often he tries to run away from the competitive situation and take refuge in avoidance behaviour.

Psychologists prescribe several techniques for improving concentration; these include yogic meditation, Zen meditation, concentration training, thought-stopping, self-hypnosis, deep breathing exercises, etc.

Motivation

Motivation has a great part to play in physical performance especially in sports. It is a process by which a person is inspired, encouraged or provided some sort of incentive to accomplish a goal-directed task such as to do his job at office well, to take part in competitive sport and achieve high success or study at school and college for a successful career in life. Without motivation it is difficult for an athlete to better his performance. Motivation involves awards, rewards or monetary benefits in some form to be given to athletes for their creditable performances and it also refers to *inner urge* for activity so that some athletes consider high sports achievement to be its own reward; they may have little regard for the material gain from playing. Motivation sustains interest in the activity; in psychological language, it is called a reinforcer of behaviour because an athlete is awarded or rewarded for his performance, he finds himself energized for a still stronger effort and works harder to improve his performance. Lack of motivation or denial of reward/award slackens effort resulting in deteriorating standard of performance. The top athletes are given awards/rewards as incentives and the professional athletes are provided with incredibly high material benefits in order to sustain their interest in the sport. The more intense the motivation, the higher the performance is an unwritten rule of sports. The relationship between athletic performance and motivation is substantial, if not perfect.

Mental Training

We know very well that in athletic pursuits mental training is as important as physical training, rather more important because it is rightly said that a game is won or lost in the mind before it is done practically. Mental training, in sporting context means many things to many people. It may mean psycho-regulation (regulating mental processes connected with physical performance) in one sense or it may denote relaxation training and stress management in another; it may involve psyching up (getting mentally aroused or prepared) or it may mean anything that influences athlete's mind for effecting performance-enhancement. To play cool (only a mentally relaxed athlete can do), to become mentally tough and ready (psyching up), and to go all out for a risky plunge (psychological training), etc., is an important proportion for all athletes. No athlete can perform optimally without training himself mentally side by side his training physically because mental training is capable of eliciting a heightened response from the body even beyond its seemingly latent limits. Mental training is a vast spectrum involving such strategies as cognitive training, perceptual training, coordination training, reaction training, rhythmic training, motivation training (goal setting), and psycho-regulation (breath control, self-instruction, imagery, autogenic training an activation). Sport is a purview of the mentally tough, determined, psyched-up and perceptually keen individual.

Spectator Influence

Spectators or crowd watching an athletic competition exert a powerful influence on the performance of athletes. Often their cheers and jeers become a deciding factor in the winning and losing of a team or an individual player. The effect of home ground or home crowd on performance is very well known to athletes and their trainers. Generally, athletes are trained to become deaf and blind to the spectators' din and noise and disturbing actions so as to remain focused on the game but this is a very difficult thing to achieve. Fan violence often erupts and disrupts the progress of a match or a performance. Many a good performance is spoiled by spectators' violence or interference. The cheers from the crowd inspire the hot favourite athletes and jeers from them dampen the spirits of their opponents. No remedy has as yet been found to this social malady.

QUESTIONS FOR EXERCISE

Short-answer Questions

Keeping the two answered-questions at the end of the Chapter : I – as your model, answer the following questions.

1. Explain how man is psychologically different from other animals.
2. Explain in your words the basis of man's behaviour.
3. Describe the three major aspects of human behaviour.

4. What is the literal meaning of the word psychology?
5. Explain briefly the concept of philosophy.
6. Why psychology could not be defined as a study of soul or mind?
7. Define psychology as it is understood today.
8. List out at least eight branches of psychology.
9. Enumerate the main features of psychology.
10. What branches of science help a talented kid to become a star sportsperson?
11. How do you define sports psychology?
12. Give at least two definitions of sport psychology from modern authors.
13. List out the salient features of sport psychology.
14. How do you get a glimpse of the personality of a person at first sight?
15. What perception of personality does a common have?
16. Though short in stature, why Lal Bahadur Shastri is still considered as a great personality?
17. Where has the word personality come from?
18. Give at least two understandable definitions of personality.
19. How did Dr. Radhakrishnan define personality?
20. List out the major dimensions of personality.
21. Why do most scientists consider personality to be a product of heredity-environment interaction?
22. Write at least four key concepts inherent in most definitions of personality.
23. Why most coaches give more importance to physical training instead of psychological training?
24. Are you convinced that physical performance is all due to physical training and not psychological training?
25. Shortlist five important factors that significantly affect human performance in sports.
26. How do our attitudes and expectations affect our physical performance?
27. Define tension and explain its origin.

28. How does tension create difficulties for the athletes when they are on the field of play?
29. What effects does a stress response produce?
30. Define anxiety and tell how it affects physical performance?
31. How does anxiety influence man's physiological and psychological functions?
32. What do you mean by *confidence* and how does it enable a sportsperson to win a game?
33. What part does concentration play in athletic competition?
34. How does a spectators' crowd influence players on the field?
35. How is mental training used in different contexts?

CHAPTER: FIVE

INTERNATIONAL SPORTS EVENTS

Games and sports are as old as the human civilization. Man is sportive by nature and it is in man's blood to be active and playful. Therefore, right from the birth of human civilization, games and sports have always been a part and parcel of man's life. All great civilizations of the world – the Indus, the Greek and the Chinese – attached utmost importance to physical activity, play and recreation generally observed as social phenomenon in the form of games and sports. It was so because games and sports:

- have served as an effective breeding ground for tough and hardy soldiers for war, which was so common those days;
- have been a source of great fun, recreation and enjoyment for the participants (athletes) as well as the spectators;
- are a symbol of social progress and cultural development in a country;
- have enabled people to enjoy flowing health, as physical exercise is next to man's biological need for water, air and nutrition;
- have helped the participants to remain physically fit and to improve the level of their fitness from time to time; and
- aim at developing sound mind through sound body.

The Greeks were the first civilized people to pay serious attention to physical education as a medium of physical fitness and character building. That was why they considered *athletics* (games and sports) as an integral part of general education and put them at par with aesthetics, ethics and mathematics in the system of their education for youth.

While the Olympic Games have had their origin in the antiquity in Greece almost three thousand years ago, the Asian Games, Common Wealth Games and Afro-Asian Games are of recent origin; they do not have a long history behind them.

OLYMPIC GAMES

In ancient times, almost three millennia ago, the Greeks had numerous athletic festivals, which included music and dance contests also. Those days Greece was not a unified nation; it was a conglomerate of scores of tiny principalities called City States, the *citizens* (persons of the Grecian race only) of which considered it their sacred duty to participate in the national sports festivals called the ***Pan-Hellenic Games,*** which were four in number: the Olympic Games, the Isthmian Games, the Pythian Games, and the Nemean Games. The Olympic Games were the most celebrated and the most prestigious of the Pan-Hellenic Games. All the four competitive festivals were scheduled in such a manner that every year some festival was organized, so that a particular festival's turn (e.g. Olympic Games) came in a cycle of four years.

The recorded historical evidence shows that the Olympic Games began in 776 B.C. and continued in a continuous rhythm of four years until 394 A.D. when Olympia - the sacred place of the Olympic celebrations - was sacked and plundered by the barbarians from the north. Later the Romans further destroyed the Greek temples and civilization. The Olympic Games had their rebirth in 1896 A.D. in Greece with the untiring efforts of a French Noble Baron Pierre-de-Coubertin. Therefore, the Olympic Games are categorized as Ancient Olympic Games and Modern Olympic Games.

The Ancient Olympic Games

The Olympic Games is one of the greatest gifts of the ancient Greece to the world imbibing in the youth the Grecian spirit of competition, freedom, democracy and brotherhood. In those days, the Games inspired people, as undoubtedly they today, with their sublime ideals and inculcated in the citizens of the Greek origin the true *Helelnic Spirit*, exhorting them to strive to develop in themselves qualities of body, mind and spirit. The ancient Olympic Games were no ordinary athletic contests they were a crowning glory of the sporting Greek civilization that has given to the entire world the light of philosophy, art, science, sculpture, mathematics, literature, so on and so forth.

Historical Background

The birth of Olympic Games is shrouded in fact and fiction of history, there being no concrete evidence as to the exact date of their commencement but the popular version puts it in the year 776 BC which is the beginning of the recorded history of the Games. So the first recorded Olympic Games are said to have had their beginning in 776 BC. The "meet moved in a rhythm of 4 years beginning as one event programme." The Greeks were sport-loving people and the games were part and parcel of their religious and cultural life.

The home of Olympics, from which the Games derive its name was Olympia, the sacred valley in Elis – a city state to northwest of Pelo Ponnese in ancient times. The place was studded with innumerable treasure houses, temples and religious buildings. The most important and most beautiful of these was the *Olympium* in the centre of which stood a giant statue of Zeus 40-feet high. Known as one of the seven wonders of the ancient world, the statue was made of ivory and dressed in robe of gold, showing the Greek god sitting in his throne.

The Greeks attached so much importance to Olympic Games that they used to reckon time by the Games and the period of four years between one and the other Games was called an Olympiad. The year 776 BC called the first Olympiad was used by the Greeks as the beginning of their chronology, but it was reckoned as the 28th celebration of the Games counting from the year 884 BC, whence the games are believed to have made an informal appearance.

There are several versions of how the Olympic Games were born. According to one, the Games were started by Hercules some where around 1253 BC. The story goes that Hercules, as a penitence for his misdeeds, was given the difficult and unpleasant task of cleansing the giant stables in which, Augeas, King of Elis, maintained a great herd of animals. He had a bet with the King that if he cleansed the stables successfully, the King would give him a big part of Kingdom. Hercules accomplished this task with the greatest ease, by diverting the river Alpheus through the stables. Augeas, however, refused to pay up, claiming that the method adopted by Hercules was all wet. Hercules then killed Augeas and took over his Kingdom, property and the animal herd. In order to purge up his guilty conscience and, at the same time, to celebrate his great victory, Hercules instituted the Olympic Games.

Another interesting version is that many centuries ago, a king of Elis, Oenomaus, had a beautiful daughter named Hippodamia. The king offered his daughter in marriage to an individual who could successfully kidnap her in a chariot. The catch was that the king would give chase in a light chariot drawn by fast horses and kill the kidnapper by hurling his spear or javelin. According to the legend, thirteen young men got away with Hippodamia but all were killed by the king after a hot chase. One day a young man named Pelops showed up to try his luck. He studied the *situation,* took certain precautions and made preparations to kidnap the princess. Pelops met the king and soon afterwards, he escaped with Hippodamia closely followed by the royal father in a speeding chariot. This time, things turned out differently. Pelops had bribed the king's charioteer to tamper with the axle of the chariot. Before the king could hurl his spear, the chariot went down in a heap. Pelops won by bribing and conquered the throne through unlawful methods and means. His conscience pricked him, and to atone for the sin, Pelops organized games and religious ceremonies on the hallowed ground at Olympia in Elis. The date generally ascribed to this episode is 884 BC.

In the third version, it is stated that constant strife among the *city states* gradually destroyed their unity and peace. Iphtius, the King of Eleira, consulted the Oracle (a predictor of future) who advised him to hold a festival of sports at Olympia in order to find peace. Though the city states could not get permanent peace, a temporary truce for ten months provided safe passage to the participants through enemy territories, and safe conduct of the Games was assured.

The Olympic Spirit

The Olympic Games formed a part of religious festival held in honour of Zeus. There was a high moral tone attached to the Games which began with an *Olympic Oath* taken by the athletes and judges before the statue of Zeus. The athletes swore to observe the rules of the contests; the judges swore to be fair; and all prayed for personal success in the Games. Through out the Games a scared flame (today called the Olympic flame) burnt at the Altar of Zeus.

The greatest honour to be attained by any Greek was winning of a simple branch of olive given to a victor in the Games. The kings competed alongside the commoners without discrimination. Even the Roman Emperor Nero (AD 68) sought the Olympic honours. Winners became national heroes. Musicians sang in their praise and sculptors preserved their strength and beauty in marble. Their feats of skill and courage were recorded by poets and writers of the time.

The Greek ideal of life was muscle-mind harmony of the highest order, which could possibly be achieved only through a strict discipline code. Winning in Olympic was a great honour and distinction which every citizen aspired to achieve. Even Plato, the greatest thinker of all times, is said to have won wrestling contests at the Games. The love of physical beauty and sense of urgency and of readiness for war constituted the background of Olympia. In the foreground was an intense competitive spirit. The competitions were not for material awards or rewards, unlike at lesser athletic meetings.

Olympia offered no prize, but a wreath of olive leaves. But that wreath was an embodiment of honour for which men contested with a kind of religious passion. Besides body prowess, the Greeks perceived the moral qualities of respect for what is due to the gods, to one's fellow men, to oneself and feeling that begets a like feeling towards oneself in others. It is the spirit of reverence, of modesty, and of courtesy.

The Golden Rules of the Games

After the ***truce*** (a temporary peace among the warring City States) was proclaimed a month before the Games, the competitors assembled at Elis to undergo final stages of training under the eyes of judges. Two days before the full moon the competitors went in procession along the sacred road to Olympia, where visitors in thousands had been assembling for days past and were now encamped upon the plains to see pageant of athletes.

No competitor was allowed to withdraw or concede a ***walkover*** to his opponent at any stage. This was severely punishable under the rules. In the beginning only the *citizens* with Greek blood were allowed to participate in the Games. The slaves were not allowed to participate. After Greece was conquered by the Romans, this rule could no longer sustain and the Romans were also allowed to compete. High moral standards were set for the competitors and a person with criminal background was not permitted to enter the contest arena.

Participation was also denied to women and the married ones could not even watch the unique sport extravaganza. Interesting as it seems, Pherenice, daughter of a former Olympic champion, Diagoras of Rhodes, disguised herself as a trainer to see her son Pesirodus take part in the contests. To her great joy her son was crowned champion and as she ran to embrace him, her robe fell off and every one discovered to their chagrin that it was a woman. Pherenice would have been severely punished for breaking the rules, had it not been that her father and brother had been Olympic champions. So, she was pardoned. To make sure that such a thing did not happen again, it was decreed that in future, the athletes and trainers would be in nude during contests. This is why the ancient Greek statues of athletes are sculptured in the nude. Only one woman could enter the stadium and she was priestess of the temple Demetra. She had a special seat at an altar opposite the seat of the judges. In all duel contests such as wrestling, boxing and Pankration, lots were drawn to match the contestants. When a competitor was left without an opponent after drawing of lots he became a reserve and took on the winner of an earlier contest.

Organisation

The organization and supervision of the Games and enforcement of rules and regulations was entrusted to the judges who also acted as umpires. The number of judges varied from time to time until 108th Olympiad (384 BC), the number was fixed as ten. The judges were elected by lots from amongst the highly esteemed citizens of Elis ten months before the Games, and the eldest of them became the chairman. The judges had the absolute power to declare the victors, and there was no appeal against their judgement except to the Parliament of Elis.

The Olympic Games started with one event consisting of a short distance sprint for lighting the flame which was used for the sacrifice to the Gods. For 28th Olympiads, (from 884 BC and 13 Olympiads from that of 776 BC - totalling 41 Olympiads) only one stadium length race called *Dromos* (approximately 103m) was held. In the 14th Olympiad the *Dianlos* was held and, on the 18th wrestling and pentathlon were added. On the 23rd Olympiad boxing was included, on the 25th *Tethrippos,* on 30th *Pankration* (a combination of boxing and wrestling) and the horse race, on 37th the race and wrestling events for youth, on the 38th the pentathlon for youth which was not held again as it was considered harmful for boys. The total number of events that were held from time to time in Olympic Games was 23. Such a number was, however, never held on any one occasion. Sometimes new events were added, and some were eliminated.

The *duration* of the ancient Olympics has been a subject of lot of controversy and difference of opinion. According to an ancient text (472 BC) the Olympic festival lasted only one day. This seems doubtful because 15 events could not have been completed in a single day. Historical evidence shows that the Games lasted five days, of which three days wee devoted to competitions and the first and the last day to religious rituals and sacrifices.

On the first day, standing before the Altar of Zeus, the athletes swore that, for ten months, they had observed the rules of training and that they would use no unfair means in the contests. Sacrifices were offered to Zeus, and it was followed by a scrutiny of the entries, and heats and ties were drawn. On the second day, the contests began with chariot races, followed by horse-race once up and down the course without saddle or stirrups. The day ended with Pentathlon, which consisted of a foot race, long jump, throwing discus, javelin throw, and wrestling before the Altar of Zeus (in all five events) meant all round athletes. The third day was the day of full moon and a culmination of religious festivals, with elaborate rituals and sacrifices in the morning. The afternoon, however, was devoted to foot races, boxing and wrestling for boys. On the fourth day the main foot races were held in the morning over courses of one furlong, two furlongs and three miles, and in the afternoon wrestling and boxing. The contests ended with a symbolic race in full armour, intending to mark the end of sacred truce. The final (fifth) day was reserved for religious sacrifices and invocations but before this, the victors were crowned.

The Decline of the Olympic Games

One of the greatest things about the ancient Olympic Games has always been that taking part is more important than winning. Although athletes incurred their own expenses and winners received many favours from their own communities and rich neighbours, they were all amateurs through and through. Unfortunately after a thousand years or so, things changed for the worse and the Olympic ideals were forgotten. The Roman professionalism, which caused dissensions and generated bad feelings, was eventually responsible for the Olympic Games becoming a battle field, instead of a friendly gathering for friendly contests of strength, power and speed. In course of time, the Olympic Games lost their moral fibre as also popularity.

The Olympic Games continued for well over a thousand years until they were suppressed by a Roman emperor Theodosius in 394 AD. Long before this, the Olympics had become degraded due to professionalism and ironically, the last recorded winner was a barbarian from Armenia. Shortly after the suspension of the Games in 394 AD, Olympia was ransacked and looted by barbaric invaders from the North, and the Romans further destroyed the Greek Temples.

The Modern Olympic Games

The rebirth of the Olympic Games, as we know it to day, was due to the devotion of a French noble man Baron Pierre de-Coubertin. He is rightly called the Father of Modern Olympic Games. Although twenty seven years before the first Modern Olympics an effort was made by Evangelios Zappas – a Greek millionaire living in Rumania – but it ended in an utter failure. Coubertin was stirred by the discoveries at Olympia and realizing the tremendous possibilities of the Olympics in a world torn and tormented by despots and the wars saw the Olympics a means of bringing people and nations together with a view to maintaining peace and friendliness among them. The spirit of Olympics conjured up before his mind's eye a pageant of youth, not of one country but of many nations. He realized that the Olympic Games stretching across national frontiers and breaking down the barriers of race, religion, colour and language, could alone establish the brotherhood of man. He conceived of Games as an instrument for promoting peace and understanding instead of being an occasion for merely suspending differences and dissensions unlike the Greek City states that observed truce during contests.

de Courbertin mobilized public opinion and presented his plans to an international congress held by French Sports Union on June 16, 1894. It was due to his earnest effort and indomitable spirit that the first Modern Olympic Games were held from 5 to 15 April, 1896 at Athens.

The Olympic Creed

The creed or guiding principle of the modern Olympic Games is a quote by Baron de Coubertin:

> *The important thing in the Olympics is not to win but to take part. The important thing in life is not the triumph but to struggle. The essential thing is not to have conquered but fought well.*

de Courbertin also had in mind the following purposes of the Games.

- To draw the attention of the world to the fact that a national programme of programme of physical training and competitive sports not only helps in developing the health of the young people but creates better citizens and promotes development of their character and personality.
- To create in them a sense of loyalty, companionship and team spirit, to enable young people to be more useful in life.
- To stimulate an urge for fine arts in the youth by organizing exhibitions and similar displays in order to broaden their outlook and make life happier for them.
- To inculcate among all sportspersons the concept that sports is a pastime and not an instrument for material gain.
- To create a spirit of international amity and good will and to contribute to better understanding among people and nations.

Based on these well-defined ideals the two fundamental principles of the Olympics are that (1) in the Olympic family there is no distinction of caste, creed, colour or race, and (2) all the competitors have to be amateurs. *An amateur is defined as a person who practices and has always practised sports through personal inclination and without deriving any material advantage whatsoever there from.*

The question of amateurism has been a matter of first serious concern and also debate with the International Olympic Committee for a long time. There have, however, been several occasions in the early stages when sportsmen quietly violating the rules of a amateurism were penalized and stripped off the medals won by them. Between the two extremes of a true amateur and undistinguished professional there are several intermediate types who can't be covered by the Olympic regulations. In view of the highly competitive nature of modern sports especially in the context of the Olympics, and the great national prestige attached to victory in the Games top athletes are gifted certain privileges such as sports clothing, transport expenses, special diet during training, long term detachment from occupational work and special attachment in military and other services.

Despite a clear definition of an amateur the code is being observed more in breach. Wilting under all-round pressure, the IOC has opened the doors for the professional sports such as lawn tennis. The ideal of amateurism is gradually disappearing from the Olympic Games for which every one at the helm of the matter - NOCs, International Sports Federations, National Governments and athletes - is to blame.

Olympic Organization and Programme

The supreme authority of the Olympic Movement is vested in the International Olympic Committee who, on its first composition, was entrusted by the Paris Congress of 25th June, 1894 with the control and development of Modern Olympic Games. Its terms of reference read as follows:

1. To cause the Games to be regularly held;
2. To see to it that the Games increasingly become worthy of their glorious history and noble ideals

(that was the inspiration of de Coubertin and his collaborators when they took up the responsibility to revive the Games).

3. To encourage the organization of amateur sporting competitions.
4. By encouraging and consolidating friendship between sportsmen of all countries, to direct and maintain amateur sport on the right road.

The IOC has only one member from each country except those countries that have had organized Olympic Games or have made a special contribution to Olympic Movement, which have two members. The IOC members elect a President by ballot from amongst themselves, who holds office for 8 years. The President can be elected for another term of 4 years. There are two vice presidents elected for a period of 4 years both being eligible for re-election. The vice-presidents and five members of the executive board are elected every four years. This nine-member body, including the president, controls the Olympic Movement and assures the holding of the games every four years.

The permanent headquarters of the IOC is located in *Lausanne* (Switzerland). The chief executive of the IOC is the Secretary General chosen by the executive board, who functions under the direction of the president. Besides the National Olympic Committees, the International Federations controlling various games/sports included in the Olympic programme are the important supporting factors in the Olympic Movement.

The IOC selects sites and dates for the Olympic Games. The honour of playing host to the Games always goes to the city, not the country in which it is located. The actual planning and organization of the Games is done by the National Olympic Committee of the country or the host city.

The ***programme of the Olympic Games*** today is very different from the one in the ancient Greece. The main difference is that the Greeks organized the contests between individuals; there were no team games, which are a modern development. In the Modern Olympics, there are several team games. Today, the Olympic programme consists of two types of games - compulsory and optional. The criterion is that a particular game must be played in at least 25 countries to be eligible for inclusion in the Olympics.

Beginning with nine events in the first Games in 1896, the figure has now gone up to 22 which is declared official by IOC. These events are the ones which are considered part of the Olympics, but the city organizing the Games does not necessary have to include all these events in the programme. The games recognized for the Olympic contests are athletics, rowing, basketball, boxing, canoeing, cycling, fencing, football, gymnastics, weightlifting, field hockey, judo, wrestling, swimming and diving, pentathlon, equestrian sports, shooting, volleyball, water polo, yachting, handball, archery, lawn tennis, etc. Besides the official games, there also are optional sport events, for which competitions can be held, but the results do not count for the purpose of ranking nation teams taking part.

The Olympic Emblem and Motto

The Olympic symbol consists of five inter-linked rings or circles representing sporting friendship of all peoples. The symbol was devised by Coubertin himself in 1913, who also suggested that it should be printed on a white flag, which should become the Olympic flag. de Coubertin proposed that each of the five rings should be different in colour - Red, Green, Yellow, Blue, and Black. Out of the five colours, at least one colour is present in the national flags of all countries of the world.

The *Olympic Motto* consists of three Latin words *Citius, Altius,* and *Fortius* meaning Faster, Higher, and Stronger. This represents the athletic goal of running faster, jumping higher and throwing more strongly.

The Cavalcade of the Modern Olympic Games

The movement of the Olympic Games through the decades has just been smooth with important events at each occasion as mentioned below;

1896-Athens (Greece)

Besides all other events, Marathon race was also conducted. The idea was to highlight an astounding achievement of an ancient Greék soldier Phillipides - who ran from the battle field at Marathon to Athens to announce the victory of Militides over the Persians in 490 BC. Philipides ran non-stop all the way, a distance of about 42 kilometres and just had time to cry out "Rejoice, we have won", before he collapsed and died. On 10th April, 1896, the highlight was the victory by native peasant Spiridon Louis in the first marathon race, which was run over the same course covered by the Greek hero Pheidippides after the battle of Marathon in 490 B.C. Only 13 nations (Australia, Bulgaria, Chile, Denmark, France, Germany, Greece, Great Britain, Austria, Sweden, Switzerland, Hungary and United States) competed in a total of nine sports.

1900-Paris (France)

The Games attracted 1,225 athletes from 26 nations and enjoyed more publicity, if not bigger crowds, than in Athens. Women players took part in the Games for the first time even against Coubertin's wishes. The Olympic motto was adopted.

1904-St. Louis (USA)

Originally scheduled for Chicago, the Games were moved to St. Louis with athletes from only 13 nations participating. The Marathon, which was run over dusty roads in brutally hot weather, was the most bizarre event of the Games.

1908-London (U. K.)

The fourth Olympic Games were certainly the wettest and probably the most contentious in history. Held at a new 68,000-seat stadium in the Shepherds Bush section of London, the Games were played out under continually rainy skies and suffered from endless arguments between British officials and many of the other countries involved - especially the United

States. The distance for the Marathon race was standardized to 26 miles 385 yards (42 km 145 m).

1912-Stockholm (Sweden)

For the first time women took part in the swimming. 24-year old Jim Thorpe, an Indian (American), from Oklahome won the two most demanding events in track and field–the pentathlon and decathlon. A year later it was learned that he had played semi-pro baseball for $25 a week in 1909 and 1910. The IOC, with the full support of the American Olympic Committee, stripped him of his medals and erased his records for violating the principle of amateurism. The medals and records were restored in 1982–29 years after Thorpe's death.

1916-Berlin (Germany)

Not held due to World War I

1920-Antwerp (Belgium)

29 countries (one more than participated in the war) sent a record 2,600 athletes to the Games. Germany and Austria, the defeated enemies of Belgium and the Allies, were not invited. The Antwerp Games were also noteworthy for the introduction of the Olympic oath (delivered in the name of the participants) and the Olympic flag, with its five multicoloured, intersecting rings as well as release of pigeons as mark of peace.

1924-Paris (France)

Paavo Nurmi, the "Flying Finn" (and the star attraction of the Games) won five gold medals, it was the way he did it. Running with a stopwatch on his wrist, Peerless Paavo captured the 1,500 and 5,000m finals within an hour of each other and set Olympic records in both. Two days later, he blew away the field in the 10,000m cross-country run where the heat and an unusually difficult course combined to knock out 23 of 38 starters (Finland also won the team gold in the event).

And finally, the next day he led the Finns to victory in the 3,000m team race. His performance overshadowed the four gold medals of team-mate Ville Ritola. Paavo broke 22 World records in athletics in his life time.

1928-Amsterdam (Holland)

The Olympic Flame was lit for the first time. A torch was lit at Olympia in Greece and carried by relay of runners to the stadium in Amsterdam to light the flame. The IX Olympiad was innovative in the sense that for the first time women were admitted to track and field (despite objections from Pope Pius IX) and gymnastics. Since this time, the Greek squad has been leading the official march past as a mark of respect to the Ancient Olympic Games. These Games marked Germany's return to the Olympic fold after serving a 10-year probation for its "aggressiveness" in World War I. The British India fielded a hockey team which won.

1932-Los Angels (USA)

37 countries sent over 1,300 athletes to the Games in southern California to compete in fourteen sports and the Games were a huge success. For the first time an Olympic village was set up to accommodate athletes. For the first time the name of a woman athlete - Madrid "babe" Didcrick - was an every one's lips. She set new records in 80m hurdles and javelin but was disqualified in high jump as she landed head long in the pit, which was considered a foul. The Japanese swept away eleven gold medals in swimming events. Just before the Games, the IOC said that Nurmi would not be allowed to participate in his fourth Olympics because he had received excessive expense money on a trip to Germany in 1929. The ruling came as no surprise in the track world where it was said, "Nurmi has the lowest heartbeat and the highest asking price of any athlete in the world."

1936-Berlin (Germany)

In Berlin, dictator Adolph Hitler and his Nazi followers

felt sure that the Olympics would be the ideal venue to demonstrate Germany's oft-stated racial superiority. He directed that $25 million be spent on the finest facilities, the cleanest streets and the temporary withdrawal of all outward signs of the state-run anti-Jewish campaign. By the time over 4,000 athletes from 49 countries arrived for the Games, the stage was set. Then Jesse Owens, a black sharecropper's son from Alabama, stole the show - winning his three individual events and adding a fourth gold medal in the 4x100m relay. The fact that four other American blacks also won did little to please Herr Hitler, but the applause from the German crowds, especially for Owens, was thunderous. Basketball also made its debut as a medal sport and was played outdoors.

1940-Tokyo (Japan)

Not held due to World War II

1944-London (England)

Not held due to World War II

1948-London (England)

Games were organized here without invitations extended to Germany and Japan. The Soviet Union was invited, but chose not to show. India participated as a free nation.

1952-Helsinki (Finland)

The Soviet Union returned to the Olympic fold in 1952 after a 40-year absence. Despite the Soviets' impressive debut, the most memorable individual performance of the Games came from Emil Zátopek of Czechoslovakia, the 10,000m champion in London; he not only repeated at 10,000m, but also won at 5,000 and in the marathon - an event he had never run before. He also set Olympic records in each race and topped it off by watching his wife Dana Zátopková win the women's javelin. Zátopek's unique triple was wildly applauded by the distance-minded Finns, but their greatest outburst came in the opening ceremonies when legendary countryman Paavo Nurmi, now 56, ran into the stadium with the Olympic torch and handed it off to another native legend Hannes Kolehmainen, now 62, who lit the flame to start the Games.The Helsinki Games virtually served to reaffirm the relations among nations and develop Olympic spirit.

1956-Melbourne (Australia)

For the first time, the Olympics were held in the Southern Hemisphere crossing over the Equator. The Soviets out-medalled the U.S. for the first time, cleaning up in gymnastics and winning their first track and field titles when Vladimir Kuts ran off with the 5,000m and 10,000m.

1960-Rome (Italy)

The Games attracted a record 5,348 athletes from 83 countries. For the first time, the organizers granted television rights for the Games to about 100 networks throughout the world. Now hundreds of millions could see the Games. Pakistan snatched the hockey gold from India who had been winners since 1928 in this event.

1964-Tokyo (Japan)

Tokyo Olympics were the most spectacular technical achievement ever seen. Computers were used for the first time successfully. The Russians left the Americans behind in medal tally. Abebe Bikila an Ethiopian won the Marathon race second time without any parallel even today. India regained the hockey gold.Twelve world and six Olympic records fell in swimming alone at the Tokyo Olympic Games.

1968-Mexico (Mexico)

Staged at 7,349 feet above sea level where the thin air was a major concern to many competing countries, the Games of the 19th The thin air helped shatter records in every men's and women's race up to 1,500 meters and may have played a role in

U.S. long jumper Bob Beamon's incredible gold medal leap of 29 feet, 2½ inches – beating the existing world mark by nearly two feet. The Indian hockey team failed to qualify for finals.

1972-Munich (W. Germany)

Some six hundred and thirty million dollars spent either directly or indirectly, made the Olympics a lavish affair. The Games were blackened by the ghastly act of a group of Palestinian terrorists from the "Black September" movement who killed two members of the Israeli athletic squad and held nine of them as hostages. The Games stopped for twenty-four hours, then, almost as a gesture to prove that the brotherhood of international amateur sport could survive the vilest blow, continued. Mark Spitz, an American Jew, showed himself as a phenomenon in swimming events winning four individual and three relay events, all in world record times.The United States also lost an Olympic basketball game for the first time ever (they were 62-0) when the Soviets were given three chances to convert a last-second inbound pass and finally won, 51-50. The U.S. refused the silver medal. Munich was also where 17-year-old Soviet gymnast Olga Korbut and 16-year-old swimmer Shane Gould of Australia won three gold medals each.

1976-Montreal (Canada)

The Games lost much of their lustre and efficacy due to political dissensions. More than thirty five African countries boycotted the Olympics on the South Africa issue. Taiwan also withdrew. When the Games finally got started they were quickly stolen by 14-year-old Romanian gymnast Nadia Comaneci, who scored seven perfect 10s on her way to three gold medals.For the first time India were relegated to seventh position in Hockey.

1980-Moscow (USSR)

For the first time the Games (of XXII Olympiad) were held in a country with a communist regime but were overshadowed by large scale boycott in protest at 1979 Soviet invasion of Afghanistan. The Games were also plagued by charges of rigged judging and poor sportsmanship by Moscow fans who, without the Americans around, booed the Poles and East Germans unmercifully.India regained hockey title (of course, in the absence of Pakistan).

1984-Los Angles (USA)

After 1932, the Olympics were held here for the second time and were remarkable for being the first privately funded affair. The Russian block except Romania boycotted the Games in retaliation for the US instigated boycott of the Moscow Games, thus making the Games "the biggest political football in the history". With four Olympic titles, Carl Lewis (USA) was star of these Games, standing equal to Jesse Owens 48 years ago. The L.A. Olympics were the first privately financed Games ever and made an unheard of profit of $215 million.

1988-Seoul (South Korea)

After 24 years (1964 Tokyo Games) the Olympics returned to Asia. For the first time all leading sporting nations (159 with athletes 9,465), except Cuba and Ethiopia, took part in the Games, which were overshadowed by the most spectacular drugs case against Ben Johnson (Canadian) who ran 100m in world's best time of 9.79 sec. Florence Griffett Joyner (USA) captured public's attention by winning three gold and one silver.

1992-Barcelona (Spain)

Political changes in Europe and elsewhere saw emergence or re-emergence of national teams on to the world sporting stage. A record 10,563 athletes from 172 nations gathered without a single country boycotting the Games. A television audience of two billion watched the most spectacular Olympic ceremonies and contests.

1996-Atlanta (USA)

A record number of 197 national athletic squads with 10,332 athletes (men and women) took part in the Games for contests in 271 events. These were the most logistically complicated Olympics to date and perhaps the most hyped and over-commercialized as well.

2000-Sydney (Australia)

A record 10,651 athletes (4,069 of them women) from 199 nations participated in these Games, the only nation excluded is Afghanistan. The doping in some cases spoiled the show.

2004-Athens (Greece)

The Game's return to their historic home ended as a surprising success. Participation records were once again broken, with 201 nations and 10,625 athletes taking part in 301 different events. While the games turned out to be more successful than many imagined, they were not without flaws. Many of the venues were awash with empty seats during major events, a stark contrast to previous games. Also, 24 athletes tested positive for performance-enhancing drugs, a reminder that today's drug culture is inescapable, even in the ancestral home of the Olympics.

2008-Busan (China)

Some 10,500 athletes representing 204 countries competed in 302 events spread out over 28 sports. China won a record 51 gold medals, and a total of 100 medals. The U.S. followed with 36 golds and a total of 110 medals, and Russia claimed 23 golds and 72 total medals.American swimmer Michael Phelps undoubtedly emerged as the star of the Games, living up to the pre-Games hype. He won eight gold medals, breaking the record set by Mark Spitz in the 1972 Summer Games. He also set a record for the most golds in a single Olympics. Phelps participated in eight events and set seven world records.The world witnessed stunning displays of athleticism, fortitude, and pageantry with few glitches or scandals to mar the grandeur.

2012-London (U.K.)

To be held

No doubt, the Olympics have come a long way with their lofty objectives, but the way things have turned out since their inception in the modern era, it is doubtful whether these objectives will ever be realized in the true spirit of the term. There have been demonstrations of racialism at several meetings, disrespect to the Olympic flag, even murders at Amsterdam and Munich, increasing drug abuse and some other tragic things, basically opposed to the spirit of the Games. Instead of becoming a meeting place for the promotion of good will, international amity, understanding and fraternity, the Olympics have become a platform for the propagation of ideologies, show of national (economic) strength and too much pomp and pageantry. Further, amateurism is being compromised and professionalism legitimized. The Olympics have already been split into two parts - the Winter Olympics and the Summer Olympics. All these things make people skeptical whether or not the Olympic Movement is striving towards the realization of its long cherished ideals.

THE ASIAN GAMES

The Asian Games were born on February 13, 1949 when representatives of Afghanistan, Burma, India, Pakistan and Philippines signed the Games' constitution at Patiala House, New Delhi and thereby becoming the founder members of Asian Games Federation. The representatives adopted *Even Onward* as the motto of the Games.

However, behind that humble beginning lies a long period of gestation on the part of the member countries plus the efforts of Prof. G.D. Sondhi, a former member of

International Olympic Committee, President of Amateur Athletics Federation of India and the prime mover behind the founding of the Western Asiatic Games.

The inspiration for the Asian Games can be traced back to two fore runners: the Far Eastern Games which were held periodically between Japan, China and Philippines in the first three decades of the century, and the Olympic Games in which the Asian countries were taking increasing interest, as well as the Western Asiatic Games (for countries east of Suez and west of Singapore), which were held in 1934, but were discontinued due to World War II.

These Games gave rise to the concept of an all Asian Games. Though the idea of bringing together the youth of Asia on the field of sports lay dormant until March, 1947, when the Asian Relation Conference called by Jawaharlal Nehru in New Delhi, presented an opportunity to bring to the notice of the countries attending that conference, the proposal for the Asian Games.

Professor Sondhi raised the question of the Asian Games project with some assembled representatives attending the Asia Relation Conference and also approached Mr. Nehru who readily offered his support for the idea. During the London Olympics in 1948, the plan was again put before a gathering of Asian representatives and the first Asian Games were initially set to take place in 1950. After several postponements, the first Games were finally held in New Delhi in March, 1951. The Asia Games have been held regularly at four years interval since then.

Originally the Asian Games Federation controlled the affairs of the Asian Games. This organization was re-named as the ***Olympic Council of Asia*** on 26, November, 1981 at a meeting of the duly accredited representatives of the affiliated Asian National Olympic Committees at New Delhi. Over the years, the Council has grown in volume and strength with 45

Asiatic NOCs as its affiliated members, the chief among them are Afghanistan, Behrain, Brunei, Bangladesh, China, Hong Kong, India, Lebanon, Malasiya, Mongolia, Nepal , Pakistan, Philippines, Qatar, Saudi Arabia, Sri Lanka, Syria, Taiwan, Thailand, United Arab Emirates, etc. The independent States of the erstwhile USSR like Kazhakistan, Uzbekistan, Ukraine etc. have also been admitted to the Asiad Movement.

Like the International Olympic Committee, the Olympic Council of Asia is the supreme body with 45 NOCS having complete authority over the organization of the Asian Games.

Official Programme

As per the constitution of the Olympic Council of Asia, the Asian Games' programme must include athletics and aquatics and art exhibitions - architecture, sculpture, painting, music etc. - as compulsory sports disciplines as prescribed in Article 19.

From out of other sports events, not less than five, shall be chosen by the organizing committee of the Games from out of archery, badminton, boxing, cycling, equestrian, fencing, football, golf, gymnastics, handball, field hockey, judo, kabaddi, rowing, shooting, squash, table tennis, tennis, volleyball, weightlifting, wrestling, yachting, canoeing etc. Demonstration of certain sports may also be arranged subject to the approval of the Olympic Council of Asia.

As is clear from the statistics of Asian Games (given on the following page) since the beginning, the number of events, participants and the duration of Games have been ever ascendant. It is estimated that the sports contest extravaganza at the Asian Games, at any point of time in history, has been second only to the Olympic Games in magnitude. This clearly indicates an ever-increasing popularity of the Games and an upward trend of the performance records in almost all events.

The following are the statistics for the Asian Games held so far:

Asiad	City/Country	Dates	No. of Nations	No. of Sports	No. of Participants Men (Women)
1st	New Delhi (India)	March, 1951	11	6	489 (31)
2nd	Manila (Philippines)	May, 1954	18	8	970 (98)
3rd	Tokyo (Japan)	May, 1958	20	13	1422 (121)
4th	Jakarta (Indonesia)	August, 1962	17	13	1545 (203)
5th	Bangkok (Thailand)	December, 1966	18	14	1945 (376)
6th	Bangkok (Thailand)	December, 1970	18	13	1752 (259)
7th	Tehran (Iran)	September, 1974	25	16	2363 (443)
8th	Bangkok (Thailand)	December, 1978	25	19	2879 (557)
9th	New Delhi (India)	November, 1982	33	21	3345 (620)
10th	Seoul (South Korea)	September, 1986	27	25	3420 (755)
11th	Beijing (China)	September, 1990	37	27	4655 (1462)
12th	Hiroshima (Japan)	October, 1994	43	34	6828
13th	Bangkok (Thailand)	December, 1998	41	36	9469
14th	Pusan (South Korea)	Sept./Oct., 2002	44	38	6714
15th	Doha (Qatar)	December, 2006	45	39	9520 (3046)
16th	Guangzhou (China)	November, 2010			

THE AFRO-ASIAN GAMES

In comparison to the Asian Games, the Afro-Asian Games are simply an infant. They are like the *blessed* kid who is born after long prayers and great labour pains. Encouraged by the stupendous success in the conduct of the IX Asian Games in November-December, 1982, the proposal for combined athletic contests of the countries of the Asian and African continents was made in April, 1983 by the Indian Olympic Association with a view to broad-basing sports in the country, and creating a much wider perspective for international exposure for sportspersons of the under-privileged countries of Asia and Africa. The proposal was put before the Association of National Olympic Committees of Africa and the Olympic Council of Asia who readily accepted it.

Historical Background

Against this background, since the proposal had come from India, the Indian Olympic Association was given the *go-ahead* to organize the Games in New Delhi. In December, 1983, the venue for the proposed Games was changed to Kuwait with the hope to hold the contests in 1985. In April, 1985 the Games were still on but in September they were cancelled, the organizers citing political instability. In 1989, the idea surfaced again with an announcement that New Delhi would host the Games in November, 1991. Once again nothing came of the plans.

The idea was brought to life again in 1999 at the end of the SAARC Games and the venue for the Afro-Asian Games was first fixed Pune and then New Delhi. On most occasions the Games were not cancelled but merely postponed until November, 2001. Preparations were slow however, and this, combined with terrorist attacks in the United States in September, 2001, caused the Games to be postponed indefinitely once again.

In May, 2002, India proposed holding the Afro-Asian Games in Hyderabad in 2003. Hyderabad was chosen as the venue because facilities there had recently been upgraded for India's National Games. The Games were finally held in 2003 from October 24 to November 2, at 8 different venues.

Organization and Programme of Sports Events

The control of the Afro-Asian Games vests in the newly established Afro-Asian Games Council whose *chief* is Sheikh Ahmad Al-Fahad Al-Sabah (the President of the Olympic Council of Asia). The organizers for the 2003-Afro-Asian Games were Government of India, Government of Andhra Pradesh, Indian Olympic Association, and Afro-Asian Games Council.

Initially, the Games were to combine the four best teams in basketball, football and handball, the four best track athletes in each event and the two best boxers in each weight class, from each region, Africa and Asia. The intent of the organizers of the Afro-Asian Games was to reward the top four finishing team and individuals from 2002 Asian Games and the 2003 African Games, and have them meet head to head. In practice this turned out to be quite difficult. So the sports programme followed the conventional route. As a result, in the first ever Afro-Asian Games, 2003, the athletes competed in 8 sports (athletics, boxing, football, hockey, shooting, swimming, lawn tennis, and weight-lifting) for 406 medals.

On a continental level, Asia won 82 gold, 80 silver, and 88 bronze medals while Africa have had in its kitty 49 gold, 41 silver and 66 bronze medals.

The performance of Indian sportspersons at the Afro-Asian Games raises the hopes of the nation for a bright future in international athletic contests. The second Games were set to take place in Algiers, Algeria in 2007. But, the Games have been indefinitely postponed.

THE COMMON-WEALTH GAMES

The Common-Wealth Games may be as prestigious as the Olympic Games for the British and its European, Canadian or Australian alleys; they do not seem to have much charm for the Asian countries that are part of the Common-Wealth because they are perceived as a means of glorification of the British Empire. The invigorating spirit that pervades the

Olympic Games or the Asian Games and enthusiasm which they generate are, perhaps, missing in the Common-Wealth Games, and yet, in any case, these contests are not insignificant from the viewpoint of development of a sports culture in the world. Organized every four years, they are the third-largest multi-sport event in the world, after the Summer Olympic Games and the Asian Games. The Games are overseen by the ***Commonwealth Games Federation*** (CGF) (CGF), which also controls the sporting programme and selects the host cities.

History of the Common-Wealth Games

The first Common-Wealth Games were held in Hamilton, Ontario, Canada. Bobby Robinson, a major influence within athletics in Canada at the time, finally implemented the event that had been talked about amongst Common-Wealth nations for over thirty years. Eleven countries with 400 athletes in total participated in the first Common-Wealth Games. Since then the Games have been conducted every four years except 1942 and 1946, due to World War II.

From 1930 to 1950 the Common-Wealth Games were known as the British Empire Games, then the British Empire and Common-Wealth Games until 1962. From 1966 to 1974 they took on the title of British Common-Wealth Games and from 1978 onwards they have been known as simply the Common-Wealth Games. A governor general represents her in the country.

The territorial jurisdiction of the Common-Wealth Games extends over countries of the Common-Wealth in Africa, Americas, Asia, Caribbean, Europe and Oceana. There are currently 54 members of the Commonwealth of Nations, and 71 teams participate in the Games. The four Home Nations of the United Kingdom - England, Scotland, Wales, and Northern Ireland - send separate teams to the Commonwealth Games,

Council of the Common-Wealth Games Federation

The control and organization of the Common-Wealth Games vests in the Council of the Common-Wealth Games

Federation, whose role stretches beyond facilitation of the Common-Wealth Games – instead the continuing success of the Games has helped to influence the outreach of the Common-Wealth and to strengthen its hands.

As a means of improving society and the general well-being of the people of member nations, the Federation also encourages and assists education via sport development and physical recreation through-out the Common-Wealth.

Underlying every decision every decision made by the Council of the Common-Wealth Federation are three *core* values - ***Humanity, Equality and Destiny.***

The vision of the Common-Wealth Games is to promote a unique, friendly, world-class Games and to develop sport for the benefit of the people, the nations and territories of the Common-Wealth and thereby *strengthen* the Common-Wealth.

Programme of Events of the Common-Wealth Games

There are a total of 31 sports (with two multi-disciplinary sports) and further 7-para-sports which are approved by the Commonwealth Games Federation. They are categorized into three types. Core sports must be included on each programme. A number of optional sports may be picked by the host nation, which may include some team sports such as basketball. Recognized sports are sports which have been approved by the CGF but which are deemed to need expansion; host nations may not pick these sports for their programme until the CGF's requirements are fulfilled. Significantly, the sports include archery, athletics, badminton, boxing, cricket, cycling, diving, fencing, gymnastics, hockey, judo, lawn bowls, netball, rowing, rughby 7's, shooting, swimming, table tennis, tenpin bowling, triathlon, water polo, weight lifting, and wrestling.

India is hosting the XIX edition of the Commonwealth Games at New Delhi from 3 to 14 October, 2010 with 17 sports, 285 events and 73 nations participating. The XX Commonwealth Games will be held in Glasgow (Scotland).

QUESTIONS FOR EXERCISE

Short-answer Questions

Taking hint from the model answers already suggested at the end of Chapter-I, answer the following questions precisely:

1. Explain the functions games and sports perform in human society.
2. What status did the ancient Greeks give to sports?
3. Explain the *spirit* working behind the ancient Olympics.
4. Throw light on the origin of the Olympic Games.
5. Where from did Olympic Games derive their name?
6. What inspired the Greeks to take part in the Games?
7. Throw light on the Greek ideal of education and physical education.
8. Enumerate the Golden Rules that governed the contests at the ancient Olympic Games?
9. Why did athletes participate in Games in nude?
10. Give your views on the organization of the ancient Olympic Games.
11. How were the events scheduled in the ancient Olympic Games?
12. Trace the reasons for the decline of the ancient Olympic Games.
13. How were the Olympic Games reborn in modern times?
14. Briefly discuss the Olympic Ideals.
15. Enumerate the purposes de Coubertin had in mind while reviving the Olympic Games.
16. Differentiate between an amateur and a professional athlete.
17. Who controls the Olympic Movement and how?
18. Give the composition of the International Olympic Committee.
19. What events/sports disciplines constitute the programme of the Olympic Games?
20. Describe the Olympic Emblem, Olympic Flag and the Olympic Motto.

21. Write a brief note on the Marathon Race.
22. Briefly trace out history of the Asian Games.
23. What is the official programme of the Asian Games?
24. How have the Asian Games been moving up the path of progress over the years?
25. Which countries have been the front runners in the Asian Games and why?
26. Why was the happening of the Afro-Asian Games postponed at least six times?
27. Enumerate the sports events included in the Afro-Asian Games.
28. To whom does the credit go for making the Afro-Asian Games happen?
29. Give the nomenclature by which the Common-Wealth Games were known over many years.
30. How do you evaluate the Common-Wealth Games in comparison to the Olympic Games and/or the Asian Games?
31. What is the territorial jurisdiction of the Afro-Asian Games?
32. Which organization controls the affairs of the Afro-Asian Games and who is its head?
33. Name a few sports events that are included in the programme of the Common-Wealth Games.
34. Compare Asian Games and Afro-Asian Games.
35. Write a short note on the role of games and sports in human life.

Appendix -I

NATIONAL SPORTS POLICY - 2001

(The National Sports Policy was first formulated in 1984 and revised in 1986, 2000 and 2001 with the twin-objective of broad-basing sport in the country and achieving excellence in international competitions. Given below is its latest version as circulated by Government of India.)

The Preamble

Activities relating to Sports and Physical Education are essential components of human resource development, helping to provide good health, comradeship and a spirit of friendly competition, which, in turn, has positive impact on the over-all development of the personality of the youth. Excellence in sports enhances the sense of achievement, national pride and patriotism. Sports also provide beneficial recreation, improve productivity and foster social harmony and discipline.

2. A resolution on the National Sports Policy was laid down in two Houses of Parliament in August 1984. The National Sports Policy was formulated with the objective of raising the standard of sports in the country. The National Education Policy, 1986 also incorporated the objectives of the policy in so far as the education sector was concerned. The National Sports Policy, 1984 provided, inter-alia that the progress made in its implementation would be reviewed every five years to determine the future course of action, as may be necessary, following such review.

3. Over the years, it has transpired that even as the National Sports Policy, 1984 encompasses various facets in respects of encouraging sports in the country, the implementation of the same is not complete and leaves much to be desired. The goals and objectives laid down in the Policy are yet to be substantially realized. A need has, therefore, been

felt to reformulate the National Sports Policy in more concrete terms, spelling out the specific measures required to be taken by various agencies, which are involved, in various ways, in promoting sports in the country.

Introduction

4. In terms of the National Sports Policy, 2001, the Central Government, in conjunction with the State Governments, the Indian Olympic association (IOA) and the National Sports Federations will concertedly pursue the twin objective of "broad basing" of sports and "achieving excellence in sports at the national and international levels". Sports activities, in which the country has potential strength and competitive advantage, need to be vigorously promoted. Towards this end, sports and physical education would be integrated more effectively with the education curriculum.
5. While the broad basing of sports will, primarily, remain a responsibility of the State Governments, the Union Government will activity supplement their efforts in this direction and for tapping the talent, including in the rural and urban areas. The Union Government and the Sports Authority of India (SAI), in association with the Indian Olympic Association and the National Sports Federations, will focus specific attention on the objective of achieving excellence at the national and international levels.
6. The question of inclusion of "sports" in the Concurrent List of the Constitution of India and the introduction of appropriate legislation for guiding all matters involving national and international jurisdiction, will be pursued.

Broad-Basing of Sports

Considering the key-role of sports in national life and for inculcating national pride in the younger generation, the objective of broad basing, that is, universalization or mass participation in sports assumes special significance. It is imperative to ensure that the educational institutions, schools and colleges in both rural and urban areas, the Panchayati Raj institutions, local bodies, the government machinery, the Sports Associations and Industrial Undertakings, as also the various Youth and Sports Clubs, including those of the Nehru Yuva Kendra Sangthan (NYKS) throughout the country are, and remain, fully associated with this programme. Efforts will be made to promote and encourage women's participation in sports. The Union and the State Governments, as well as the Sports Federations will endeavour to promote a "club culture" for the speedier development of sports in the country.

8. In the National Sports Policy, 2001, high priority will be accorded to the development of sports in the rural areas to harness the available talent and potential. In this context, the Village Panchayats/Gaon Sabhas as well as rural Youth and Sports clubs will be mobilized to facilitate development of the requisite infrastructure and for the identification of talent through an appropriate competition structure in the rural areas as also in the disadvantaged and remote parts of the country including North East which appear to merit special consideration under various schemes. Efforts will also be made for tapping such potential as for swimming in coastal areas and archery in tribal areas. The available talent will be nourished and actively supported. Geographically disadvantaged regions will be extended additional support for the promotion of sports. There has been a strong tradition of indigenous and traditional games in practically all parts of the country through ages. Indigenous games will be promoted through schemes related to rural sports.

Integration with Education

9. The integration of Spots and Physical Education with educational curriculum, making it a

compulsory subject of learning up to secondary school level and incorporating the same in the evaluation system of the student will be actively pursued. A National Fitness Progamme will be introduced in the schools of the country, steps initiated to augment the availability of infrastructure, including play fields/sports equipment and action taken to provide physical education teachers in educational institutions through, inter-alia, the training of selected teachers in these disciplines. Specialized sports schools may also be set up. An appropriate inter-school and inter-college/university competition structure would be introduced at the national, state and district levels.

Infrastructure Development

10. The availability of adequate sports facilities throughout the country is basic to the development and broad basing of sports. In addition to the Union and State Governments, the sustained involvement of other agencies, including the Panchayat Raj Institutions, Local Bodies, Educational Institutions, Sports Federations/Associations, Clubs and Industrial Undertakings will be enlisted in the creation, utilization and proper maintenance of the sports infrastructure. While existing play fields and stadia, both in rural and urban areas, will be maintained for sports purposes, the introduction of suitable legislation may be considered for providing open areas to promote sports activities. Steps would be taken to evolve low cost functional and environmental friendly designs in this regard, so that maximum benefits could be derived through relatively low levels of investment. Efforts will also be made to optimally utilize the available infrastructure and manpower and special coaching camps organized, during the vacations, to provide

intensive training to talented sport-persons, even as they pursue their academic work.

Excellence in Sports

11. The Union Government will focus attention on achieving excellence in sports at the national and international levels. Various sports disciplines will be prioritized on the basis of proven potential, popularity and international performance. Particular emphasis will be placed on the development of such priority disciplines and prioritization reviewed, from time to time. The IOA and the State Governments would accord higher priority to such disciplines. In planning the development of various disciplines, the genetic and geographical variations within the country would be taken into account so that in area of potential, in particular disciplines, timely steps could be taken to harness the existing and emerging talent. Centres of Excellence will be set up to identify and train outstanding sports-persons including sport academies where young and talented sports-persons will be groomed to achieve higher levels of performance in the international competitions.

National Sports Federation (NSFs)

12. It is recognized that the management and development of sports are the function of the Indian Olympic Association and the National Sports Federations, which are autonomous bodies and who, in turn, have affiliated state level and district level associations. The Government and other concerned agencies and the Federations/Associations have, therefore, to work together harmoniously and in a coordinated manner to fulfill the objectives of the National Sports Policy, 2001. At the same time, the Indian Olympic Association and various Sports Federations/Associations will need to demonstrate

orientation towards the achievement of results and ensure tangible progress in the field of sports, keeping which in view, model bye-laws/organizational structures may be formulated for the NSFs, in consultations with them, and with due regard to the Olympic Charter, so as to make the functioning of the Federations/Associations transparent, professional and accountable.

13. Acknowledging the importance of national championships for developing competitive spirit and for talent scouting, it would be incumbent on Federation/Associations to hold Annual Championships in various disciplines in all categories viz. seniors, juniors, and sub-juniors (for both men and women) at the district, state and national levels. Each National Federation would draw up the Annual National Calendar of these events sufficiently in advance, every year, which would be compiled and published by the IOA. Greater emphasis would be placed on promoting the development of sports amongst the juniors and sub-juniors and more talented amongst them identified for special sports training and support.

14. Effective participation in international events, especially the Olympics, Asian and Commonwealth Games, is a matter of national pride. Participation in these events has, so far, largely been restricted to those disciplines in which creditable performance is anticipated. The contingents to represent the country in such events need to be chosen in due time, in the light of performance and promise in the National Championships and else where. Long Term Development Plans (LTDPs) will be prepared for each discipline, incorporating details of standard of performance, targeted levels of performance, participation in competitions in national and

international levels, sports exchanges, scientific support and the holding of international competitions in the country. The implementation of the LTDPs will be reviewed periodically and the same would be continued, as a rolling plan year after year. The release of the Government assistance would be considered on the basis of performance relating to the LTDP in question.

Scientific Back-up to Sportspersons

15. The significance of scientific back up to sports stands well established. Accordingly, action will be initiated to strengthen this area, in accordance with the international standards. Experts would be associated with each sports discipline or groups of sports disciplines, on a continuing basis, to provide requisite support in terms of nutrition, psychology, medicine, pharmacology, physiology, bio-mechanics and anthropometrics as well as other branches of sports sciences. Suitable mechanisms would be introduced to achieve coordination between the laboratory and the field, that is, between the coaches and the sports scientists, and particular care taken to ensure nutritional support to talented sports-persons and to sustain their mental health and competitive spirit.
16. Appropriate research and development measures will also be initiated for the promotion of sports and to impart special skills to promising sports-persons so that they are enabled to give out their best in the international and other prestigious competitions. The SAI and the NSFs would take coordinated steps towards the modernization of the infrastructure required for the training of sports-persons and to provide them with the scientific support for achieving excellence in sports.

Sports Equipment

17. Suitable measures will be initiated to ensure access to sports equipment of high quality. While the approach to import of equipment would, not doubt, bear the long term interests of the indigenous sports goods manufacturers in mind, the import of raw materials as well as finished goods of international quality should be permissible to under Open General Licence. Similarly, Sports Federations/Associations and other recognized organizations involved in sports promotion, as also eminent sports-persons, may be extended exemption from customs duty. The matter relating to exemption from Sales Tax for sports goods and free movement of raw materials and finished goods in the country would be pursued with the State Governments.

Training and Development of Coaches, Sports Scientists, Judges, Referees and Umpires

18. The Policy recognizes that the standards of coaching as scientific back up in the country and those pertaining to umpires, judges and referees need to be upgraded. Concerted steps will be taken to train Coaches, Sports Scientists, Judges, Referees and Umpires, in line with the international standards. In addition to developing such expertise on an international basis, within the country, the deputation of promising persons to training courses, conferences, seminars, workshops and tournaments abroad, so that they remain abreast of relevant developments in their fields, will be encouraged. Coaches would receive rigorous training for up-gradation of skills and may also be deputed overseas for the purpose.

Incentives to Sportspersons

19. Incentives provide recognition and financial security to distinguished sports-persons, during and after their sports careers, and also motivate the youth in

the serious pursuit of sports activities. Adequate assistance will be extended for insurance cover and medical treatment in the event of such eventuality/ requirement. Job reservation for sports-persons as per the prescribed categories will continue.

20. Social recognition, the conferment of awards and honours at the national, state and district levels, incentives in the form of cash awards and avenues of employment will be important elements of the National Sports Policy, 2001. Alongside sports-persons, suitable incentives will be provided to coaches, judges and referees for developing skills and enriching their experience.

Sports and Tourism

21. The Policy recognizes the inter-dependence and inter-relationship between the sports and tourism sectors, the integrated development of which is capable of generating very substantial revenues and ensuring a high volume of tourist traffic from within the country and from overseas, while simultaneously promoting a sports and fitness culture in the country. Adventure sports, in particular, have great potential for the promotion of tourism. Toward this end, the concerned Ministries/Departments of the Union and State Governments, that in those handling sports, tourism and related subjects, will have to draw up joint/united plans and proposals for various parts of the country, with due reference to the possibilities in the north eastern region, and to execute these programmes in a systematic and coordinated manner.

Resource Mobilization for Sports

22. Insufficiency of financial resources has been a major constraint in promoting sports in India. While the Union and the State governments would need to provide higher budgetary provisions, special efforts are equally called for to mobilize corporate funds for

the development of sports in the country. Accordingly, corporate houses would be approached and encouraged to adopt and support particular disciplines as well as sports-persons in the longer term. For this purpose, tripartite agreements between the Government and the concerned Sports Federations and the Corporate Houses may be entered into for different sports disciplines. The context of policy of economic liberalization, the private/corporate sectors would be more closely involved with the promotion of sports, in general, and to build up and maintain sports infrastructure, in particular, with requisite emphasis on the latest technologies. A suitable package of incentives may also be evolved for this purpose. Eminent sports-persons of established merit will be encouraged to set up and manage sports academies.

23. It may be recalled that a National Sports Development Fund has been created with initial contribution of the Union Government. All contributions (from within and outside the country) to this fund have been extended 100% exemption from income tax. The mobilization of resources for this fund will be strenuously pursued and the feasibility of exempting the incomes of sports federations and sports-persons (sources other than employers) from payment of income tax explored.

24. The revenues generated by the sale of broadcasting television rights of sports events will be shared between the concerned sports federation/ association and the broadcasting agency, public or private, on mutually agreed terms, through appropriate revenue sharing arrangements.

Mass Media

25. The role of mass media is central to the popularization of sports amongst the people at large. The electronic media, including the national

broadcasters, the private channels and the print media would be suitably mobilized for strengthening a sports culture in the country.

Globalization

26. As a resurgent India confidently enters the New Millennium sports and related activities will be increasingly utilized as medium for promoting cooperation and friendship in the region, as also globally. Sports for sports-persons and coaches, scientific support, the latest research aids and development of infrastructure, and earning laurels for the country, in sports and games, on the other.
27. The National Sports Policy, 2001 would be reviewed, periodically in order, inter-alia, to incorporate changes/modifications which may be necessitated by technological and other advancements in the field of sports.

Note: *In 2008, an attempt was made by the Government of India to recast the National Sports Policy and a draft in the shape of Comprehensive National Sports was brought out and discussed and debated at various forums but it could not be finalized due to stiff opposition from the Indian Olympic Association and its affiliated National Sports Federations on account of certain proposed provisions, for example, establishment of a regulatory authority to coordinate all sport effort in the country. Hence, the whole exercise to finalize the new policy and implement it was suspended and the Central Sports Administration reverted to the 2001 version of the National Sports Policy.)*

Appendix -II

NATIONAL SPORTS AWARDS

In order to broad-base sports, attractive more and more people to sports and motivate sportspersons as well as to honour them, the Government of India have instituted a variety of sports awards over time. Most of the State Governments too have followed suit and have come out with similar kind of sports awards as incentives. Maharana Partap Award in Rajasthan Maharja Ranjit Singh Award in Punjab, Chhatrapati Shivaji Award in Maharashtra, Ek-Lavya Award in Madhya Pradesh etc., are examples of the State Awards bestowed upon outstanding sportspersons besides the cash awards of various value.

The major National Sports Awards are as given below.

ARJUNA AWARD

Named after Arjuna - the legendary hero of the Mahabharata, known for his inimitable skill, strength and marksmanship as an archer - the *Arjuna Award* was instituted by the Government of India in 1961 as a token of the highest national recognition to distinguished sportsperson(s). The Award is given every year on the recommendations of the recognized national sports federations and in accordance with the criteria laid down by the Ministry of Youth Affairs and Sports, Government of India. The Arjuna Award carries a bronze statuette of Arjuna with a drawn bow aiming at the target, a scroll, a blazer with monogram, a necktie, and a cash prize of Rs. 5,00,000.00 The award is presented to the sportsperson(s) for consistently outstanding performance during the previous three years of their active sports career. In some cases it has also been conferred on the old-timers as a *lifetime achievement award*. In general, one sportsperson is selected for the award from each recognized game/sport for his/her individual performance of exceptional order. There is no bar, however, on more than one sportspersons especially women being honoured with this prestigious award in one game/sport.

The conferment of the Award is decided by a duly constituted committee by the Government of India after a thorough scrutiny of the recommendations received from different national sports federations. A national sports federation is permitted to recommend a maximum of three cases for the award but the selectors may pick up only the most meritorious individual from out of those recommended; another, however, can be a woman which is an exception. The ultimate decision lies with the Government. The Arjuna Award is *not* to be conferred twice. It can be withdrawn if the awardee indulged in such acts as are prejudicial to the interests of sports and/or the State. The Award cannot be challenged in a court of law.

RAJIV GANDHI KHEL RATNA AWARD

The *Rajive Gandhi Khel Ratna Award* was launched in 1991-92 for the spectacular and outstanding performance in the field of sports by the sportsperson(s) in a year (Apri1l to March 31). The award carries a cash prize of Rs. 7,50,000.00 a scroll of honour, and a plaque. In case the Award is to be conferred on more than one person in a team event, the amount shall be half the amount for each person, the scroll and the plaque.

The major objective of the award is to honour the sportspersons, to enhance their general status and dignity, and get to them a place of honour in the society. This award may motivate the upcoming and continuing sportspersons to give out their best in sports competitions, and intensify the spread of sports culture in the country. Proposal for the award may be sent to the Ministry of Youth Affairs and Sports by members of Parliament, State Governments, Sports Authority of India or National Sports Federations giving full details of achievements of the sportsperson(s) at national and international levels, recommended for the Award. The final decision on the award is taken by the duly constituted committee of the eminent sportspersons/sports administrators of long-standing and unimpeachable integrity whose decision is final and binding on all, and cannot be challenged in a court of law.

The Award is given to the individual(s) only once in life time, and may be in addition to the other award(s) which the individual(s) might have won. The Award may be cancelled if it is proved that the awardee has obtained it through fraudulent means or misrepresentation of facts or has not conducted himself honourably subsequent to the date of the conferment of the Award.

The recipients of this prestigious Award are Vishwanathanan Anand, Sachin Tendulakar, Dhanraj Pillai, Anju Bobby George, Rajyawardhan Singh Rathore, Manavjit Singh, Saina Nehwal, and others.

DHYAN CHAND AWARD

The Dhyan Chand Award for Life-Time Achievement in Sports and Games (instituted in the name of world-acknowledged *Hockey Wizard* Major Dhyan Chand) was brought into existence in 2002 and is a recent addition to the list of National Awards instituted by the Government of India. The Award is meant to honour those sportspersons who have contributed to sports by their performance and continue to contribute to promotion of sports even after their retirement from active sports career. The Award also carries a cash award of Rs. 5,00,000.00, a plaque, and a scroll of honour.

Some of the outstanding awardees have been Ashok Dewan, Brig. Labh Singh, Manoj Kothari, Rajinder Singh (Jr.), Satish Pillai, Kuldip Singh, etc.

DRONACHARYA AWARD

Dronacharya - the legendary court teacher of the Kaurva and Pandva princes of the Mahabharata fame - was responsible for producing an ace archer like Arjuna and the invincible club-fighter like Duryodhana besides several other warriors of eminence in the art of war and sport. He is said to have no comparison in war-skill teaching, wisdom of the ancient scriptures, and use of celestial weapons. The Dronacharya Award named after this great *Guru* is a big tribute to the universal teacher who has the power and skill to transform an insignificant speck into a performing blaze in any art of excellence, sport no less.

Instituted in 1985 by the Government of India, the Award is meant to honour eminent coaches who have successfully guided the destinies of individual sportspersons or teams and caused them to achieve outstanding results in recognized international sport events during three years preceding the conferment of Award. The Award carries a cash prize of Rs. 5,00,000.00, a citation, and a plaque. The major objective of the Award is to honour the coaches and motivate them to put in spirited efforts in improving the standard of performance of sportspersons in the best tradition of the Indian culture.

The Award is given every year according to the well-laid out criteria. For example, a coach whose athlete(s) or team, in a recognized game/ sport, have won medals at the Olympics, Common Wealth Games, Asian Games, Asian Championships, or World Cups or World Championships during a span of three years, and/or obtained medals in international fixtures. The award may also be conferred on a coach who has coached player(s) or team to the level of excellence in an indigenous game for three years. Some of the outstanding coaches who received this Award include O.M. Nambiar, O.P. Bhardwaj, Desh Prem Azad, Bal Bhagwat, Guru Hanuman, A.K. Kutty, and others.

MAULANA ABBUL KALAM AZAD TROPHY FOR SPORTS EXCELLENCE

Instituted as *Running Trophy* in 1956-57 by the Government of India, the Maulana Abbul Kalam Azad Trophy *for sports excellence* is awarded annually to the University which has given the best all-round performance in games and sports during the year of award. This coveted Award carries a cash of Rs.10,00,000.00 (to be utilized for acquiring sports equipment), and a replica of the Trophy.

Since its inception, the Trophy has been Guru Nanak Dev University, Amritsar for 21 years or so and three times in a row recently by Punjabi Univesity, Patiala.